Katherine Anne Porter and Texas

KATHERINE ANNE PORTER AND TEXAS

AN UNEASY RELATIONSHIP

Edited by Clinton Machann
and William Bedford Clark

TEXAS A&M UNIVERSITY PRESS
COLLEGE STATION

Frontispiece: The celebrated portrait of the writer in the early 1930s, photographed by George Pratt Lynes. Courtesy Lynes Estate

The paper used in this book meets the minimum requirements
of the American National Standard for Permanence of Paper
for Printed Library Materials, Z39.48–1984. Binding materials
have been chosen for durability.

LIBRARY OF CONGRESS CATALOGING-IN-PUBLICATION DATA
Katherine Anne Porter and Texas : an uneasy relationship / edited by
    Clinton Machann and William Bedford Clark.
            p.   cm.
        ISBN 0-89096-441-6 (alk. paper)
        1. Porter, Katherine Anne, 1890–1980 — Knowledge — Texas.
    2. Porter, Katherine Anne, 1890–1980 — Homes and haunts —Texas.
    3. Authors, American — 20th century — Biography.   4. Texas in
    literature.   5. Texas — Biography.   I. Machann, Clinton.   II. Clark,
    William Bedford.
    PS3531.0752Z716   1990
    813'.52 — dc20
        [B]   89-20667
                                                                      CIP

FOR
Alena, Tessie, and Sarah
AND
Mary and Eleanor

Contents

Illustrations

Acknowledgments

THE PRESENT VOLUME grew out of a symposium held on the campus of Texas A&M University in the spring of 1988. Made possible in part by a grant from the Texas Committee for the Humanities, the symposium also enjoyed the generous support of the Interdisciplinary Group for the Historical Study of Literature, the College of Liberal Arts, the Women's Studies Program, and the Department of English at Texas A&M. The editors wish to thank the following individuals for securing the necessary institutional support for the conference: Daniel Fallon, Arnold Vedlitz, Hamlin Hill, Larry J. Reynolds, Katherine O'Brien O'Keeffe, Jeffrey N. Cox, and Harriette Andreadis. Joan Givner, Lewis P. Simpson, and Patricia P. Perini offered invaluable advice during the planning stages. Much of the success of the symposium must be credited to the Advisory Committee, consisting of Sylvia Ann Grider, Sally Dee Wade, Mark Busby, Janis P. Stout, and Jody Bates. Mark Busby, W. Craig Turner, Deborah J. Barrett, and Frank E. Vandiver brought distinction to the symposium program through their participation. We wish to acknowledge the generosity of Dr. Herbert L. Wade and the cheerful voluntarism of Thomas Wilmeth, Delma Porter, Tanya Long, Suna Purser, Susan Egenolf,

Gary Lovan, Lisa Lovelace, Leslie Kennedy, and Leslie Sogandares.

Blanche T. Ebeling-Koning and her colleagues at the University of Maryland—along with Paul Porter—deserve special thanks for locating and making available to us the photographs reproduced in this volume. On behalf of our contributors we would like to generally acknowledge the use of Porter materials in Special Collections, University of Maryland College Park Libraries.

The editors are especially grateful to Isabel Bayley, Katherine Anne Porter's literary trustee, for permission to print the letters that accompany Cleanth Brooks's memoir.

CLINTON MACHANN
WILLIAM BEDFORD CLARK

Introduction

A Folklorist Looks at Katherine Anne Porter

SYLVIA ANN GRIDER

THE FEUD between Katherine Anne Porter and her home state was long and lively. Born at Indian Creek, Texas, and buried there beside her mother, she chose to live most of her adult life elsewhere. For long periods she was estranged from members of her family, and she reacted to the snubs of the Texas literary establishment with outbursts and diatribes. In her fiction she denied or reconstructed the realities of her early life in Texas. On their side, the Texas literati made it clear that they preferred their writers to be rugged males. The Texas Institute of Letters, when making its first award, passed over the finely crafted stories of its prodigal daughter in favor of a macho native strain, and the University of Texas trifled with her pride by first promising (she thought) and then refusing to name its humanities research library in her honor. Porter's emotional attachment to her home state fell victim to the cowboy mentality that has traditionally proclaimed Texas a fine place for men and horses, but hell on women and oxen.

The feud between Porter and Texas still has not been fully reconciled. Though she made a private peace of her own before her death in 1980, the estrangement and the puzzle have remained. This volume is a major step toward understanding, if not closing, the rift.

The conference from which most of the essays in this collection are drawn was held April 21–23, 1988, on the campus of Texas A&M University. Funded by the Texas Committee for the Humanities, the College of Liberal Arts, the Department of English, the Interdisciplinary Group for the Historical Study of Literature, and the Women's Studies Program, the conference sought to examine the uneasy relationship between Porter and Texas. Significantly, it was held at a place other than Austin — the scene of the most inflammatory incident in the vexed history of Porter's tension with her native state.

This was the third conference devoted exclusively to Porter and her work. The first was the 1976 symposium at Howard Payne University in Brownwood, Texas. The second conference, "The Katherine Anne Porter Memorial Lecture Series," was held at the University of Texas at Arlington on April 11, 1984, as the first of an ongoing annual series of lectures devoted to fiction. The speakers at the 1984 conference were Cleanth Brooks, George Hendrick, and Dorothy Walters.

The invited papers of the 1988 symposium, presented here in a different sequence, clustered around two themes: Personal Recollections, and Porter and the Transfiguring Imagination. Two other essays — by Willene Hendrick and Janis P. Stout — which were not presented at the conference are included here because they expand on conference themes and thus round out the inquiry into the Texas aspect of the life of Katherine Anne Porter.

Willene Hendrick's memoir opens the first group of essays, revealing her experience of the difficulty of trying to untangle Porter's early life story through fieldwork and interviews. Cleanth Brooks and Paul Porter in turn fondly relate their personal recollections of a dear friend and a beloved relation. The second group of essays brings the discord and estrangement into sharp focus. Joan Givner's eloquent plea challenges Texas to accept Porter and welcome her home. In the next essay, Don Graham compares Porter favorably with those he classifies as the "lesser" Texas authors. Thomas F. Walsh and Janis P. Stout examine the hold Texas had on Porter's imagination and how that hold is expressed in certain of her creative works. Finally, Darlene Harbour Unrue categorizes and evaluates the various sources of and influences on Porter's work. The collection concludes with Sally Dee Wade's select, annotated bibliography of primary and secondary materials specifically involving Porter and Texas.

Although Porter spun a largely fabricated tale of her life, especially regarding her family and Texas roots, the facts now are clear, thanks in large part to the meticulous biographical research of Joan Givner. The chronological skeleton of the Texas relationship is as follows:

1890   Born at Indian Creek, Texas.

1892   Mother dies; family moves to Kyle, Texas, to live with paternal grandmother.

1901   Grandmother dies; family moves to San Antonio.

1906   Marries J. H. Koontz of Inez, Texas.

1914   Leaves Texas to work in movies in Chicago.

1915   Divorces J. H. Koontz.

1917   Works for a Fort Worth newspaper.

1918   Leaves Texas for Denver.

1921   Spends a few more months in Fort Worth.

1936   Returns from extended residence in Europe to visit Texas and her mother's grave.

1937/38   Spends winter in Houston.

1939   *Pale Horse, Pale Rider* published; rejected by Texas Institute of Letters.

1944   *Leaning Tower* published.

1959   Misunderstands intentions of University of Texas regarding the naming of new library after her.

1976   Howard Payne University holds symposium in honor of her eighty-fifth birthday.

1980   Dies; buried next to mother at Indian Creek.

Porter's childhood and adolescence in Texas were filled with rural hardship and hand-me-downs. She experienced none of the genteel poverty she describes so vividly in her fiction. Motherless, with a father who wouldn't work to provide for his children, life for Porter in Texas was hardscrabble and impoverished. She seems to have spent the rest of her life trying to make up for what she was deprived of as a child.

The seemingly irreconcilable rift between the adult Porter and Texas came as a result of two specific snubs, one very real and the other perhaps only perceived but not intended. Although she departed Texas in 1914, returning only for occasional visits, she left not because of any particular disaffection with her native state, but rather to escape a miserable marriage and to create her own, self-fulfilled life and career. This decision to leave Texas in order to create a life for herself is the precursor to Amy's powerful assertion in "Old Mortality": "if I am to be the heroine of this novel, why shouldn't I make the most of it?"[1] Porter made the most of it for the rest of her life, writing stories based on an early personal life history that she fabricated. Porter was indeed the heroine of her own fictive life, a "novel" she wrote best when she was geographically farthest from Texas. Or, as Janis P. Stout says in her essay, Porter's best fiction results when she "combines estrangement with nostalgia."

Nearly twenty-five years after her escape, and after she had achieved national recognition as a writer, her stunning collection of short stories *Pale Horse, Pale Rider* (1939) was passed over by the recently organized, male-dominated and establishment-oriented Texas Institute of Letters in favor of the decidedly inferior *Apache Gold and Yaqui Silver* of a favorite son, J. Frank Dobie. The reason for the selection? Ostensibly, the institute had deferred to the more "indigenous" nature of Dobie's subject matter but, more to the point, Dobie had chosen to live and write in Texas, rather than to leave, as Porter and so many others had done.

This slight lies at the heart of the "uneasy relationship" between Porter and Texas. No matter how much acclaim her writing achieved outside Texas, the self-conscious literary and intellectual establishment of the state refused to acknowledge that a woman writing about a nonstereotypical image of Texas deserved any recognition whatsoever. They simply ignored Porter. To some extent, as Joan Givner points out in her essay, this negative attitude toward Texas women writers, including Porter, prevails even today. But in 1939 Porter was the *only* living Texas woman writer of any significance. The only other Texas woman writer to gain national recognition, Dorothy Scarborough, had died in 1935, and the writings of fellow Texans Ruth Cross and Karle Wilson Baker never received national recognition. The snub directed toward Porter was perceived as personal, primarily because of her gender and unconventional lifestyle. The continued critical acclaim of *Pale Horse, Pale Rider,* along with the relegation of Dobie's *Apache Gold and Yaqui Silver* to the status of general Texana or juvenilia, accentuates the injustice of the institute's rejection of Porter.

The other rift between Porter and Texas occurred twenty years later, in 1959, when through an apparent misunderstanding, the University of Texas did not name its new library after her. She was furious, insulted, and hurt. Had this episode been handled differently, the 1939 slight by the Texas Institute of Letters could have been exonerated and the rich collection of Porter papers and memorabilia would have been deposited at the University of Texas instead of the University of Maryland. Furthermore, Porter would likely have lived out the rest of her life in Austin, in the home she had sought throughout her life. The intellectual loss to Texas of this Porter legacy is immeasurable.

In spite of the institutional rejection of Katherine Anne Porter by Texas, she never hesitated to acknowledge her Texas roots and the emotional bond the state held on her. Many of her best stories are redolent with Texas images and references. "Old Mortality," "Noon Wine," "Pale Horse, Pale Rider," the

"Old Order" sequence, "Holiday," and, somewhat obliquely, "The Leaning Tower" all have strong Texas associations.

In many respects, she had made her *personal* peace with Texas a few years before the institute's rejection of her work. In 1936, after an extended period of living abroad, Porter returned to Texas for a family visit. As described in Joan Givner's biography, Porter and her father made a sentimental pilgrimage to the small, weed-choked cemetery at Indian Creek that held her mother's grave. Porter was so moved by the experience that she wrote a poem to commemorate the occasion and decided that she wanted to be buried next to her mother.[2]

Then, a year or so later, Porter returned to Texas again, writing at one point in a letter, "My father and I visited the dreary little place at Kyle, empty, full of dust, decayed, even smaller than I remembered it. I had no feeling at all. I never lived there really, and have not any memories that I cannot bring up, look at, and put away again calmly." According to Joan Givner, the visit to Kyle "was marked by a calm acceptance of her past. She saw houses and gardens and children who had once been herself, and she had no regrets and no wrenchings of the heart for any part of the past. Everything had 'moved back and taken shape' and was 'something whole and finished,' and she could look at it 'with complete detachment except for a pleasurable sense of possession.'"[3]

Scholars and critics, of course, have made much of the fictionalized, Southern belle past which Porter claimed as her own. In her stories as well as her personal reminiscences, the ties to Southern aristocracy, the flamboyant and indomitable ancestors, and the dignified home-place are all part of a past that never was. To a literary critic, such prevarication is perplexing and fraught with dark psychological overtones. But from the perspective of the folklorist, such fabulation of a personal past is more easily understood and accepted.

A narrative genre that has recently come under intensive scrutiny from folklorists is the *family saga*, the collective folk-memory of a family's ancestors and history. The genre was first recognized and named in 1958 by Porter's fellow Texan and contemporary, Mody Boatright, in an article entitled "The Family Saga as a Form of Folklore."[4] As many subsequent articles and studies have made clear, most families remember their past not as it really was, but as it ought to have been or might have been. Through constant and communal retellings, the stories achieve a decidedly literary structure and polish — a process that has little to do with empirical truth. But unlike Porter, members of undocumented and everyday families don't have professional biographers trying to ferret out every detail of their past lives. The fabulated stories, with their modifications and adaptations, remain intact and unchallenged within the limited circle of family oral tradition, where they function to validate family values, dreams, ambitions, and longings. If ancestors are invented along the way or settings and dates changed, no one objects as long as the general contour and emotional core of the story remain.

Although historians disparage these family stories because of their lack of verifiable, empirical data, the stories nevertheless manifest a family recognition of past influences on the present, whether the events happened in one's own family or to someone else or whether they even happened at all. This process may be responsible, in part, for the elaborate tale Katherine Anne Porter spun about her family's past. The primary difference is that Porter's family saga was individually rather than communally created and told. As far as we know, no other member of her family subscribed to the fanciful genealogy and family heritage she created. Even so, family members may have contributed unknowingly to the process. For example, according to Givner, Porter's sister once wrote to her that "she was feeling nostalgic and homesick — *not for things that were but for things that should have been.*"[5] We know from friends and admirers that Porter was an accomplished raconteur who could hold an audience spellbound, no matter how many times they had heard her tell the story before. Consciously or unconsciously, Porter brought to bear all of her artistic skills on this elaborate family saga, and the lasting legacy lies in her formal fiction, especially the Miranda stories. The fact that early biographers took many of these stories at face value is tribute to the skill with which she imagined this past that never was.

In light of this tendency to fabulate, one cannot always be sure whether to trust Porter's own interpretation of how and why she remembered the past in the creative way that she did. But one of her comments, an extensive excursus in her essay "Noon Wine: The Sources," has been singled out by several of the essayists in this volume as providing significant insight into Porter's attitude toward her Texas past. In that passage, here quoted in full, she says about that "place of memory":

My time in Mexico and Europe served me in a way I had not dreamed of, even, besides its own charm and goodness: it gave me back my past and my own house and my own people — the native land of my heart.

This summer country of my childhood, this place of memory, is filled with landscapes shimmering in light and color, moving with sounds and shapes I hardly ever describe, or put in my stories in so many words; they form only the living background of what I am trying to tell, so familiar to my characters they would hardly notice them; the sound of mourning doves in the live oaks, the childish voices of parrots chattering on every back porch in the little towns; the hoverings of buzzards in the high blue air — all the life of that soft blackland farming country, full of fruits and flowers and birds, with good hunting and good fishing; with plenty of water, many little and big rivers. I shall name just a few of the rivers I remember — the San Antonio, the San Marcos, the Trinity, the Nueces, the Rio Grande, the Colorado, and the small clear branch of the Rio Blanco, full of colored pebbles, Indian Creek, the place where I was born. The colors and tastes all had their smells, as the sounds have now their echoes: the bitter whiff of air over a sprawl of animal skeleton after the buzzards were gone; the smells and flavors of roses and melons, and peach bloom and ripe peaches, of cape jessamine in hedges blooming like popcorn, and the sickly sweetness of chinaberry florets; of honeysuckle in great swags on a trellised gallery; heavy tomatoes dead ripe and warm in the midday sun, eaten there, at the vine; the delicious milky green corn, savory hot corn bread eaten with still-warm sweet-milk; and the clinging brackish smell of the muddy little ponds where we caught and boiled crawfish — in a discarded lard can — and ate them, then and there, we children, in the company of an old Negro who had once been my grandparents' slave, as I have told in another story. He was by our time only a servant, and a cantankerous old cuss very sure of his place in the household.[6]

In this loving description of a halcyon childhood, Porter has blended her memories of Kyle with the ambience of San Antonio, where she attended school. According to local residents, people in Kyle did keep Mexican parrots for pets and the "soft blackland farming country" really was full of "fruits and flowers and birds." Porter's memory falters, however, with the mention of her birthplace, Indian Creek, which is ecologically quite different from Kyle. The peaches and Cape jessamines and crawfish of the passage are in Kyle, not Indian Creek. Here Porter's memory is accurate but selective; she simply records all of her childhood memories as though she is speaking of a single, wonderful place, omitting whatever does not fit.

To further examine this point, in her essay Willene Hendrick quotes Porter as having said that "she would never get over her love for the place she knew where camellias and figs and gardenias (Cape jessamines) and peaches and watermelons and azaleas and honeysuckle all grew out in the open with a few lemon and orange trees." Hendrick then goes on to offer her own insight into Porter's glowing recollection: "In memory, Porter often romanticized the native land of her heart when she talked about it. What we saw on the banks of Indian Creek where the Porters lived were mesquite and dry bluestem grass.

The Porter garden and orchard were very likely beautiful in spring and fall, but citrus trees have not grown in Brown County in recent centuries."

Again, in this passage, Porter is referring to Kyle, not Indian Creek. According to local tradition, a horticulturist from Philadelphia introduced citrus trees into the Kyle region and even developed a hybrid lemon/lime to flavor his favorite mixed drinks. Citrus trees are also fairly common in San Antonio.

Porter's long-delayed reconciliation with Texas finally came at the end of her long and troubled life. Howard Payne University in Brownwood, near where she was born, held a symposium to celebrate her eighty-fifth birthday. She attended as guest of honor, read from her works, and even handed out the diplomas at commencement. During this event, the only official Texas acknowledgment of her greatness during her lifetime, she seems to have made her peace after having been slighted for so long. As an article in the *Dallas Morning News* summed it up: "There was a feeling as she read that something had come full circle for Katherine Anne Porter on this day. A pattern had been completed, all loose ends gathered and tucked in, and nothing lost."[7]

Since that magic day in Brownwood, the slow healing process of Texas' acceptance of Katherine Anne Porter has begun. A new generation of scholars and writers is replacing their Dobie-trained forebears, and some of them (Larry McMurtry and his *Lonesome Dove* notwithstanding) are looking beyond the cactus, sagebrush, and cowboy stereotype of Texas literature. For example, in a recent list of the fifty most influential Texans, Porter is listed but Dobie is not.[8] In 1982, A. C. Greene chose *Pale Horse, Pale Rider* as one of the "fifty best books on Texas," calling it "the best Texas fiction ever written."[9] Texas' literary provincialism may at last be waning.

Finally, prompted in part by Joan Givner's remarks at the 1988 conference, at least one group of Texas citizens has undertaken negotiations with the Texas Historical Commission to place state markers in Kyle, Porter's childhood home, and in Indian Creek, the site of both her birth and burial. Once these markers have been erected, they will represent Porter's Texas history as it was, not as it "should have been."

NOTES

1.   Katherine Anne Porter, *The Collected Stories of Katherine Anne Porter* (New York: Harcourt Brace Jovanovich, 1965), p. 189.

2.   Joan Givner, *Katherine Anne Porter: A Life* (New York: Simon & Schuster, 1982), pp. 295–96.

3.   Givner, *Life,* p. 303.

4.   In *Mody Boatright, Folklorist,* ed. Ernest Speck (Austin: University of Texas Press, 1973), pp. 124–44.

5.   Quoted in Givner, *Life,* p. 423 (emphasis added).

6.   Katherine Anne Porter, *The Collected Essays and Occasional Writings* (New York: Delacorte, 1970), pp. 470–71.

7.   Joan Givner, ed., *Katherine Anne Porter: Conversations* (Jackson: University Press of Mississippi, 1987), p. 191.

8.   *The Roads of Texas* (Fredericksburg, Texas: Shearer Publishing, 1988), n.p.

9.   *The 50 Best Books on Texas* (Dallas: Pressworks Publishing, 1982), p. 33.

Part One
Personal Recollections

Indian Creek: A Sketch from Memory

WILLENE HENDRICK

LATE IN AUGUST, 1962, my husband and I set out from the hamlet of Santo, between Mineral Wells and Stephenville, where we had been visiting, to find the obscure town of Indian Creek, where a certain well-known writer had been born in a log cabin. Indian Creek was not on our road map, but the *Texas Almanac* showed it as a tiny dot south of Brownwood. When we neared Brownwood, we stopped at a truck stop to have some coffee and ask directions. As we paid, we asked the waitress. She thought for a time, then asked a construction worker who was just coming in.

"Let's see now," he said. "Indian Creek. Well, it's off that way," and he pointed to the south. "Best way to get there is to go to that new school up there on top of the hill, turn down that new highway they're puttin' in up there, go two, three mile and then turn right again on a little paved road. You'll see signs from there on."

They looked at us curiously, as if nobody in recent times had asked directions for the Indian Creek settlement. We didn't explain that we were on a literary excursion.

"You can't miss it," he called as we headed for our car.

But we did, easily. The paved farm road forked often. There

were no signs. Finally we were on a dusty, washed, bumpy road. We took each turn with new uncertainty, gazing down the dwindling tracks leading through the fenced farmland, nowhere.

When the sign came, it was a battered wooden one, home-made-looking, saying "Indian Creek Baptist Church" and pointing to a large peeling white frame building, which looked like a barn. We took the blind road left and soon found a red-brick structure, looking like a schoolhouse but saying "Indian Creek Methodist Church" in large concrete letters across the front. We looked around for a likely house where someone might live who would know something about the Methodist church records, for we knew Harrison Porter, the author's father, had been the Methodist Sunday school superintendent, and we thought it likely that there were still several people around who knew where Katherine Anne was born and remembered the Porter family. Some years earlier, Donald Stalling, working on a master's thesis on Porter at Texas Christian University, had found such locals.

From the road in front of the Methodist church, we could see a small two-story frame house, a battered, abandoned general store, a brick and stone gymnasium with its roof now gone, a prosperous-looking large frame house, and, down a side road, a small brick house and a metal shack.

It was in that last building made of tin and iron that we found the church secretary, a lady of about seventy. She had never heard of the Porter family, and she said that even if any records of births and deaths had been kept seventy years before, they had all been destroyed, because something had happened to the church before her time: a fire or a storm had destroyed it. She sent us into the country to see two elderly ladies she thought might remember the Porter family.

Her directions were clear, and within a few minutes we arrived at the McBride house. We walked across a sandy yard and were met at the front door by Mrs. McBride's daughter. We ex-

Katherine Anne with her father, Harrison Boone Porter, on a pilgrimage to her mother's grave at Indian Creek. Courtesy Special Collections, University of Maryland College Park Libraries

plained that my husband was writing a book about Katherine Anne Porter and that the Methodist church secretary had sent us to see Mrs. McBride.

"Oh, yes," she replied, "she knew them, the Porters. She's out in the fields now. Went for a little walk, out to see my husband and take him some water. She ought to be back any time now. She'll come back for her dinner."

We asked if Mrs. McBride would mind talking about the Porters. No, the daughter didn't think she'd mind; she did have some papers and things. The daughter left us to see if she could find those papers, and in a few minutes she returned to the front porch, where we were seated in the swing, not with papers but with a medium-sized woman whom she introduced as Mrs. McBride. We explained our mission again.

"I didn't really know the Porters too well," Mrs. McBride began. "Mostly I remember when they left here. There was an auction. They sold all their things. I was there, I remember. We bought the churn. Somebody bought the high chair. With the baby sitting in it. But it wasn't the baby you wanted to know about. Katherine Anne was a little girl. Pretty little girl, I remember, running around all over everywhere, with little black curls."

"Can you tell us anything about her? Or the Porter family?" we asked.

Mrs. McBride paused to think about the distant past, and her daughter broke in.

"That Miss Porter, she came not long ago, with her father. They were looking for her mother's grave. Went up to the cemetery to see it. Took Mrs. Porter's picture from the tombstone. The picture was sealed in glass and stuck to the stone. I guess they did it. It's gone now." (It was sometime later that we learned that the visit of the Porters characterized as "not long ago" had actually taken place in May, 1936.)

Mrs. McBride remembered something in a dresser drawer, went into the house, and returned with a photograph, a pic-

The author's mother, Mary Alice Jones Porter. She died when Callie (the future Katherine Anne) was not quite two years old. Courtesy Special Collections, University of Maryland College Park Libraries

The photograph discovered by Willene Hendrick at Indian Creek, showing Callie Porter (seated on her mother's lap) in the company of her siblings Annie Gay and Harry Ray Porter. Courtesy Special Collections, University of Maryland College Park Libraries

ture of the Porter children. We saw immediately that the smallest, the baby sitting on a woman's lap, was Katherine Anne. The eyes were hers, and the mouth, and the defiant look. The mother's face had been omitted by the photographer. Was Mrs. Porter already too ravaged by illness to allow her face to be shown? Or was she removing her face to emphasize the children? Or was there some other reason?

"The picture was with my mother's things. Mrs. Porter must have given it to her," Mrs. McBride said. We gazed at the picture, trying to read its messages. On the front, stamped across the bottom, we read "Cheapest Gallery, Brownwood, Texas."

"You can have it, that picture, if you want it," Mrs. McBride said.

"But wouldn't you like to keep it?" I said, startled by the offer.

"No. I don't want it. I didn't ever know them, not really. They moved away when I wasn't any bigger than that oldest girl there," and she pointed to the picture of Annie Gay Porter, then about five or six. "No, I don't want it. They warn't no kin to us. Yes, you take it. Send it to Katherine Anne if you don't want it. I understand she writes books now."

There was a pause. "You are writing a book," she said to my husband. She sounded tired, as if she had nothing more to say to us. "Miss McAden can tell you a whole lot more than I can. She was older when the Porters left."

As we were leaving, we said we would send the picture on to Katherine Anne Porter (and we did). Then we drove down a dusty road to Miss Leola McAden's house. When we arrived, she was just leaving the dinner table. She was a bird-like little woman, and she was glad to have company. She talked to us for over an hour about all she could remember from her childhood about the Porter family. Yes, she remembered the Porters well, but mostly she remembered her own childhood and family and warned us often to keep her from straying away from what we wanted to know. She remembered Harrison Porter as a kind and gentle man. And Katherine Anne, whom

Porter (left) *with her sister Mary Alice and grandmother Catherine Anne Skaggs Porter, the family's matriarch. Courtesy Special Collections, University of Maryland College Park Libraries*

the Porters called Callie; Miss McAden called her Callie too. She thought that was Katherine Anne's christened name, but it was a long time ago, and she had never seen the Porter family Bible with its lists of births and deaths. There had been fishing expeditions with Harrison Porter and the children. She could show us their favorite spot. The Porter house had stood near the creek; she could take us to the very spot, but it was a mite warm to take a ramble in the middle of the day, so she pointed it out to us from her porch. The Porter log house was long gone. The McAdens, like Mrs. McBride's family, had bought some of the household goods at the auction. They now owned what had been the Porter farm.

"Do you by chance still have anything from the house?" I asked.

"Oh, no," she replied. "It's all worn out long ago."

We talked and talked. She let us go, finally, reluctantly, talking all the way out the door, across the yard, and she was still talking as we drove away.

She had told us how to get to the dusty, weed-grown, grass-covered cemetery. There we found Mrs. Porter's tombstone, with its inscription: "Dearest Loved one, we have laid thee / In the peaceful grave's embrace, / But thy memory will we cherish / Till we see thy heavenly face." We also found marks on the stone indicating that a photograph could have been removed from it, but we could not be certain of that. Mrs. Porter's death date on the monument revealed a problem in the Katherine Anne Porter biography—Porter for years had given the year of her birth as 1894, but Mrs. Porter had died in 1892.

Putting aside the biographical problems we had uncovered —we know now that Porter was born in 1890 and that she was christened Callie Russell—what came out of that day-long excursion was a sense of desolation calling into question Porter's declaration that "she would never get over her love for the place she knew where camellias and figs and gardenias (Cape jessamines) and peaches and watermelons and azaleas and honey-suckle all grew out in the open with a few lemon and orange trees." In memory, Porter often romanticized the native land of her heart when she talked about it. What we saw on the banks of Indian Creek where the Porters had lived were mesquite trees and dry bluestem grass. The Porter garden and orchard were very likely beautiful in spring and fall, but citrus trees have not grown in Brown County in recent centuries.

As we left Indian Creek that day, we heard the echo, "She warn't no kin to us." We asked then, "Where are your people, Katherine Anne Porter? Who are they?" Now, over twenty-five years later, and with much recent scholarship, including Joan Givner's masterful biography of Porter, it is clear how complete was Porter's sense of rejection in Indian Creek and in Texas by "her people." Her talent turned that rejection, with its intense emotions and insights, into remarkable artistry. Is it not now time to claim her as "our kin," our own?

The Woman and Artist I Knew

CLEANTH BROOKS

I FIRST MET Katherine Anne Porter in 1937, at Allen Tate's. She was soon to be moving to New Orleans, and then to Baton Rouge. My wife and I really became acquainted with her in Baton Rouge. Indeed, soon after she came, she lived in an apartment just across a narrow corridor from the apartment in which we lived. The result is that we saw her literally every day for a year or so. While I was away at the university—I was teaching at this time at the Louisiana State University—she was trading recipes with my wife or exchanging comments about radio programs or the state of the country as World War II was obviously approaching. Indeed, she and my wife soon became fast friends.

Miss Porter at this period was not doing very much writing —hardly any, I should say, save for letters. She was on a great domestic binge in which she was enjoying cooking, taking rides, housekeeping, exchanging recipes, reading a great deal, and so on. As one can tell from her stories, she was a great conversationalist, and we much enjoyed her stories about her earlier life in Mexico when the great revolution in painting was going on there; about her brief encounter with the movies in

Chicago where, I believe, she played some bit parts; about her life in Greenwich Village, Paris, and Berlin.

Among other things, she talked fairly often about her early life in Texas. She was not defensive about it. In fact, she indicated that she thought that she had not grown up in a wholly backward region, that there were books to read and opportunities to see some plays given by touring companies and to become acquainted with music. In short, she was never pointedly hostile toward her native state, nor did she feel that she had grown up in a kind of cultural wasteland. I grant that she usually spoke in rather general terms. I did not take notes — saw no need to take them. I was not intent on writing her biography. But I did form the impression from my talks with her, as well as from reading her stories, that this woman had not come up out of a totally deprived childhood. Her vocabulary was too good; her knowledge of the language, of people, and of social customs and manners just too detailed and intimate for it to have been any other way.

Biographers from outside may very well have the illusion that Southerners not in comfortable circumstances had no cultural advantages. But such people, I think, do not realize the relative lack of class distinctions in the South and how many families who regarded themselves as people of good stock and good breeding had been reduced to what, according to present standards, would be regarded as underprivileged conditions. After all, the Civil War left a devastating economic heritage on the South. As for my own growing up, though I was never particularly conscious of the fact, I can see now that we were reared in what I can only call something like genteel poverty.

This is not the place, however, to debate how circumstantial and detailed in fact Katherine Anne's accounts of her early life — or her later life, for that matter — were. She did like to embellish a story. I think she did it often unconsciously, and she *was* a wonderful storyteller, as her own short stories, themselves obvious fictional accounts, duly testify.

When Katherine Anne's last marriage broke up, as it did fairly shortly, she was to leave Baton Rouge, but she and my wife kept up a correspondence, particularly in the years soon after she left. The letters I shall present here were mostly written to my wife. They will reflect far better than any account of my own something of the personality of the gracious and spirited woman we knew during the late 1930s and early 1940s. Her letters show her artistic gifts, but they also display her wit, her sense of humor, her pride in her own abilities, her gift for friendship, and other aspects of this very complex, and in many respects most delightful, woman.

In the years following her departure from Baton Rouge, Katherine Anne Porter lived in a variety of places, in a number of which we visited her in later years. I shan't attempt to give a full serial list, but the places would include Santa Barbara, California; Saratoga, New York, where she was rehabilitating an old house with a great deal of charm near Saratoga Springs; and a residence in downtown New York City, of which she had two floors of a large building (other floors were sublet). She also was for a time at the University of Virginia in Charlottesville and later in Washington, D.C. Before this, she lived at least two or three years in Georgetown, just outside of downtown Washington. For several years she lived in Connecticut, though we saw too little of her while she was in the state. She did not live close to where we did, and since she did not drive she was less accessible.

The many changes of address I think show something about her. She was perpetually—so it seems to me as I look back on her life—a wanderer, a seeker, a person looking for the bluebird of happiness and the one happy valley in which she could be truly at home.

On the whole, she kept up a rather buoyant heart and showed an uncomplaining front to the world, but my wife told me of more than one occasion when Katherine Anne confessed to her a deep despondency, in which she felt that her life had come to nothing. Romantic as she was in personality, I suppose that her hopes were really unattainable. Yet she was always undaunted, looking for the happiness that lay just out of sight but which she was sure she would eventually find. Each new house or flat she took possession of was going to prove the perfect one, and I think her change of houses and her incessant movings about the earth in search of the perfect place in which to put down roots reflect her quest for the perfect lover, the husband who would be everything to her, the husband whom, of course, she never found.

In a sense, hers was a rather tragic life, so it seems to me.

One of the reasons that Katherine Anne so cherished success, as indeed she did toward the end of her life — literary success, fame — was the fact that the real happiness she wanted had always eluded her. But no one knew better, I am sure, than Katherine Anne, in her heart of hearts, that the literary fame and the wealth that eventually came to her with her novel *Ship of Fools* could in no way compensate for what she had sought so long and painfully, and had missed.

To her romantic attitude toward life she joined flightiness of judgment. I do not mean that she lacked intelligence or alertness. Such was not her weakness. But her judgment was surely flighty, if I may use an old Southern expression. In spite, however, of both these attributes and her passionately emotional nature, how classical is her art. I do not mean to disparage it by calling it classical. It is anything but cold and lifeless. On the contrary, it is warm and spirited, but classical in the sense that every word counts; that the form is beautifully, though unobtrusively, present; and that her stories have a proper beginning, a middle (that is a development), and a satisfying ending. The paradox of romantic heart and classical art remains for me the essential way in which I have to look at this remarkable woman and her equally remarkable work.

The letters that follow, of course, are a selected portion of the very many letters she wrote to my wife. Let me add that I have edited them, lightly, choosing things which reveal Katherine Anne best and suppressing or disguising the names of some of the people mentioned. I do so, not because there is anything scandalous in the letters, but because my wife thought one ought to be very careful in exposing private papers of any sort. She would not have wanted me to reveal the names of real people, some of whom, or their relatives, are still alive. At any rate, here are the letters.

Yaddo, Saratoga Springs
October 14, 1940

Dearest Tinkum [Edith Amy Brooks],

I have a very fine letter from you at about the same time you will be having a fairly silly one from me. The returned clipping reminded me I had written before, for some reason I forgot sending it entirely.

. . . .

It is true that A.____ is a saint, and saints must have very special tests and trials provided for them. God sent him a plague indeed, and I suppose good Christians should bless their plagues as a sign of God's love. That is indeed the Catholic doctrine as opposed to the Protestant which teaches that God sends you health and prosperity if you are a good boy or girl. It is strange though, Tinkum, about virtue on the grand order: it can touch and impress people mysteriously, and they may not even know what the attraction is. People at [a certain college] hung around ____, impressed, respectful, really loving him, and not being able to say why. He seemed, and indeed no doubt was, completely unconscious of the effect he had on them.

. . . .

My own memory of the Pontalba is that I did very little work on week-ends. All things considered, work would have been a sheer waste of time. . . . I wonder who [X] thinks he is fooling? Virgil Thompson hit the nail on the head when he remarked simply that "sculptors are stupid." I never knew many, but I never knew a bright one. As for the painter, it would be heaven's own blessing if he took permanently to sailor's dives, his wife's stepfather would

die, and she could go back and run her plantation in Alabama
as God meant her to. There is a waste of good qualities if ever I
saw it.

Yaddo, Saratoga Springs
May 5, 1941

Dear Tinkum,

Your letter was gorgeous, but the notes that stick in my mind
and horrify my imagination are those about the methods of petty
crime employed by [X] and [Y] in order to become "pure" artists.
Starting out at this late day to purify themselves is to confess they
have always been impure. A pure artist is pure from the beginning, at least in intention and in practise [*sic*] so far as he is able,
and he always knows when he fails. It is like living a virtuous life
on any other plane: you may not be up to it, but if you stop trying, you are damned. They seem a little late, to me. My Catholic training reminds me that it is never too late to mend and God
will accept your sincere repentance on your death bed; but Art
is not so forgiving. The worst of it is their befuddlement about
morals. I remember stories of my old Wobbly and radical friends
in Mexico, who stole bottles of milk off backsteps of little poor
houses in the towns they were bumming through, and stole fruit
and bread from little street stands where poor men were trying
to make a living: and they roared with laughter, saying they called
it sabotaging the Capitalist system. . . . I remember Gene Lolas
telling me how his anti-clerical friends used to sit on cafe terraces
and made obscene remarks to nuns passing by, to manifest their
anti-clericalism.

Yaddo, Saratoga Springs
October 11, 1941

Dearest Tinkum,

Your letter arrived this morning just before Sunday dinner, so
I just read the story of [Y] and the servant problem in the deep
south to Newton Arvin and Colin McPhee (composer) who were
my table companions. WE [*sic*] whooped with pure glee, it was a
beautiful yarn, and I felt too that it was a kind of real glimpse into

a real southern point of view (yours) that Arvin (Indiana) and Colin (Montreal) would probably never have had. A precious letter, darling, it has made my day.

My beautiful house is hungry as any growing child, and keeps the cupboard bare. I had planned as well as I could to keep a tiny margin between me and downright want, but it just closed up suddenly with me caught fast in the vise. . . . However, money came suddenly and went again as suddenly, but made a difference, a great and happy one . . . [she describes progress on the house restoration]. In my weaker moments I sometimes wonder why such natural and simple things as I want and need are so very hard to come by, but I am very willing to work for what I want and do pay cheerfully for it so long as I can possibly manage. . . . It seems most wonderfully worth doing, what else would I want to do? I can think of nothing, quite literally. For the first time in my life I can't see — don't want to see, wouldn't accept for a moment — any second choice, any alternative.

. . . .

Yaddo is not exactly open, but not closed either; it has taken on its winter compromise, with a few last leaves lingering, and I seem to be the lastest [*sic*] leaf of all. I now occupy a fine big south room in the back of the mansion, with bath and dressing room. The rest of the place is closed, except for the servant's parlor and dining room with a small kitchen attached, downstairs. This is used as a public passage way. I also make fires there in the fire place and get my own coffee in the morning. Then Arvin, McPhee, Elizabeth and I go over to the garage and eat in the kitchen, upstairs, and the men are nested down in little shacks in the woods, and I inhabit this entire fifty room place alone. It is so big and impersonal I never think about it, and sleep here in perfect ease of mind, as remote as if I were a hundred miles from anywhere at all. Elizabeth lives in her own house, her sister Marjory in hers, Old Madam Pardee, 87 years old, lives in the big house where Mr. Peabody used to live (she was the secretary and companion to Mrs. Trask and has been right here for about sixty years), Leonard Erlich has moved to North Farm and hardly ever shows up, he is there by himself, as I was last winter, and indeed, the housing situation at Yaddo is about as lavish as anybody could ever want. It really comes of Elizabeth's profound feeling that every human being needs at least eight walls and fifty acres between himself and every other human being, but you will see us struggling from various points of the landscape towards a common center with a good deal of eagerness, sometimes; we are not as Olympian by half as Elizabeth would have us believe.

She is the real Olympian, but the rest of us are just little clay-footed creatures who need to snuggle up to each other now and then.

Yaddo, Saratoga Springs
January 20, 1942[1]

Dear Cleanth,

The issue (re VWB et all [*sic*]) is precisely what you say it is, and what has been done to the Southern Review is precisely the sort of thing that school of thought would like to do to all such as we. . . . Will indeed use the war as pretext, excuse, and shield. . . . Oh boy, have I got sumpin to say? Tell me more or less how many words. I imagine two thousand would be enough. . . .[2]

. . . .

The Yeats number is magnificent, the real word for it. Nothing better could be imagined, and everybody seemed at his high level best. As usual I admired Zabel, heavens, what a civilized mind it is; T. S. Eliot was intelligent and cagey, Blackmur, Ransom, Burke, Tate, oh well, ALL of them, simply hauled off and made a first rate job of it. This sun does set in glory.

One thing strange: that refrain "I am of Ireland And the Holy Land of Ireland" which runs like the basic theme through the whole collection of essays, haunted me from the first, it makes my hair rise. It was the point of that poem, the reason for its beauty and meaning, and I thought it was the greatest refrain Yeats ever wrote. . . . And at this late day my ignorance is rebuked; I don't mind, ignorance *should* be rebuked — but for some reason it made me happy to learn that that song was old and known and part of the common memory of Ireland; I'm glad Yeats didn't write it, for this way, it belongs to everybody. . . .

I could love Yeats if only because he loved Dean Swift. I am apt to be fond of persons who are fond of (1) St. Augustine, (2) St. Francis, (3) Joan of Arc, (4) Sir Thomas More, (5) Dr. Johnson, (6) Dean Swift. Why are those my particular loves and heroes? Some of them would gladly have burned some of the others at the stake. But I feel some mystical quality, or element, common to all of them, maybe I could name it, but it is enough to know that it is there. . . .

> Boulder, Colorado
> July 8, 1942

Dear Tinkum and Cleanth,

I hope you will be pleased (and perhaps confirmed in your deepest opinion of me) when you learn that I am really a scoundrel. I busted my contract with Sarah Lawrence and took up with L. S. U. just like any hussy looking around for the highest bidder. The term is shorter, too. There seemed everything on earth to recommend it, and the more I thought about S. L. the gloomier I got. It goes Bennington one better in progressiveness, and one is not even supposed to advise the young what to read or to look for. She is supposed to browse around and pick out her own education. Myself, I was nobody's nitwit when young and I had very advanced notions of what I wanted to learn and to do: but the fact remains that my notions were based very soundly on an early acquaintance with great literature and great art and music, and a stern training in theology and morals. All that had been soaked into me almost before I knew it: it was in the air, in the bookshelves, and in the minds of my elders. . . . At Sarah Lawrence they study Clifford Odets for drama, for instance. Perhaps morals didn't stick with me, but a lot of other desirable things did, just the same.

Well, as you know, L. S. U. makes no pretense of fostering literature or the arts, but on the other hand nobody will care if you suggest that the young might investigate the sources of literature a little. I fancy the military authorities there rather feel that this year they can taper off with me, and perhaps next year the whole repellant [*sic*] subject of creative writing can just be dropped altogether. . . . We'll see. I truly believe that a little, subversive quiet knot of people working darkly as a unit in a hostile place, can get more real work done than ever they could in the broad shallows of a place like Sarah Lawrence.[3]

Liege, Belgium
December 5, 1954

Dear Tinkum and Cleanth,

Morton Zabel wrote me from London, and then Paris, and gave me the news about you — news to *me*, I mean — about how you had been in Italy last spring. You know what an exurberant [*sic*] traveler he is, so he gave me a wonderful sunny impression of the whole thing; and also rather a melancholy feeling of being very far away from my friends — not that I am not always off in some unfrequented spot trying to make a living. Well, this is the unfrequented spot to put an end to that sort of thing, I should say.

. . . .

This Gothic North about gets me down; but I remember that I was got down once before by the Gothic North, and this time I intend to resist to the last. Everything is solid here, solid, solid, even the skies — thick sultry blue and smoky greys; wild howling bitter wind for days at a time, then cold wicked rains, and then just days of darkness when you keep the curtains wide open and the lights on at once — not that there any lights to speak of. Now and again, things clear up, the sun breaks through for an hour, and there is the most beautiful shimmering watery light, and you see just what the old Flemish Masters saw; sometimes I walk out in the strange clair-obscure like twilight, though it is midday, with the wind blowing, and I have a kind of Hallowe'en excitement; but if I let myself think at all, I ask myself *what* I am doing here. . . . I know well enough, practically speaking. And I think, when I get through running back and forth to Brussels on errands of one kind or another, and have run the last errand here buying dreary little household clutter to make this place habitable, and the last visit to this bureau and that trying to get the carte d'identite settled, and the reading at Antwerp over; and the holidays, and two more speaking engagements at Brussels: I *think* I am going to have time to work a little. . . . Well, I have never been so disengaged from a place or occupation in my life as here: if I were disembodied on a desert island I couldn't be more not-present. I haven't seen a soul I'd ever want to see again, and I am sure it is my fault — there are some extremely nice people around. . . . The Americans around in strategic places are just the usual run of the mill clutter — Oh GOD where do they come from?

> Ridgefield, Connecticut
> August 8, 1958

Tinkum darling, It's a good thing I'm not a Calvinist because by now I'd be forced to admit I had sinned away my day of grace. I am trying to make a last triple copy of this you-know-what [the manuscript for *Ship of Fools*], and the time is so short and the art so long, I get benumbed now and then. And I've GOT to do it now, because I start the new Virginia chore, and besides a full season of readings, from Portland, Oregon to Portland, Maine, Auburn, Alabama to Poetry Center, New York, Corcoran in Washington, and others I can remember [*sic*] without looking in the date book. So I see no end to this bedeviled life until it itself ends. . . . I can't come for a visit, I wish I could. You'll just have to come to Virginia, darling — wouldn't you and Cleanth like that, for a little change?

The weather is really earthly paradise here, and I couldn't be more pleasantly located. But the worm in the bud is here, too: I carry my own supply. But I still believe I'm going to send this ms. out finished before I leave. . . .

> Love, Katherine Anne

NOTES

1. Isabel Bayley, Katherine Anne Porter's literary trustee, writes: "With regard to the letter dated January 20, 1942, Miss Porter, on my photocopy of the original, has crossed out 'January 20, 1942, Yaddo, Saratoga Springs' and written (I recognize her hand-writing) 'Yaddo, January 9, 1942' underneath."—WBC, Ed.

2. The *Southern Review,* edited by Cleanth Brooks and Robert Penn Warren, had become a major force in international letters since its inception in 1935 and had brought unprecedented distinction to its host institution, Louisiana State University. Nevertheless, the university's administration decided to discontinue support for the quarterly, citing in part the reassignment of resources brought on by World War II.—WBC, Ed.

3. Katherine Anne Porter did not get to Louisiana State University after all.

Remembering Aunt Katherine

PAUL PORTER

O NCE UPON A TIME in Hollywood an interviewer asked my cousin Ann what it was like living with Katherine Anne Porter. After some reflection, Ann replied with a shrug, "It's like living with your favorite aunt, that's all."

I want to say a few things about the same aunt, who was my favorite, too. Nothing scandalous, nothing arcane about the symbolism or provenience of her fiction.

My first memory of Katherine Anne Porter is from the time she visited Houston in 1936, when I was a timid sixteen. This meeting took place at a family gathering in the home of her sister, Mary Alice, known to me as Aunt Baby. My clearest memory of Aunt Katherine that evening, almost my only memory, is of a small, silver-haired woman, very animated, smoking a great deal, with a fascinating voice and a mysterious accent. She wore a sleeveless white piqué evening gown made from a design by Schiaparelli. No jewelry, *but* . . . her earlobes were rouged! Astonished, her sisters and the other ladies made indulgent little jokes about it among themselves. Of course they had rouge on their cheeks, Aunt Baby quite a lot of it, but they thought rouged earlobes were outlandish, unseemly, just the kind of thing you would expect of someone who went off to live

in Paris and exposed herself to the well-known wicked habits
of the French. If Aunt Katherine was aware of what they were
saying, she ignored it; and she rouged her earlobes for the rest
of her life.

I believe it was in 1938 when we met again. She had taken
rooms, a kind of railroad flat, in a big clapboard house in Houston Heights, not far from where I lived. She had no telephone,
so I just walked in on her, intruded, you might say, although
she never did. I was totally enchanted. Everything about her
seemed different, meaningful, glamorous — a word she hated,
by the way. We looked together through a massive book of
Audubon's bird paintings; she made my first avocado and
bacon sandwich; she had a whale-bristle hairbrush; there were
magical piles of books and manuscripts I longed to look at; and
she and the whole apartment were redolent of marvelous soaps
and powders and perfumes. One day she played a little trick
on me. She pretended that she had lost a coin under a tall wardrobe and asked me if I would retrieve it for her. Down on my
hands and knees, I found my face only a few inches from the
glaring eyes and gaping jaws of a very alive-looking stuffed alli-
gator. She burst into laughter when I fell over backwards, then
kissed me when she saw that I was embarrassed, and said that
she was sorry. At once it was all right, and we laughed about
it together. Another time, a budding young know-it-all, I reared
back and said that the music of Chopin was just too simple to
be taken seriously. She explained to me that one of the hard-
est tasks of the artist was to make his hellishly difficult and complicated art appear simple and clear. She promised me that
someday we would listen to Chopin together when she had her
phonograph records, which were somewhere in a warehouse,
as her possessions so often were. I asked if she had *Ra*vel's
*Bo*lero. Without wincing at my blunder, or blushing at her lie,
she said yes. I thought, Gee! she must have every record in the
world. In an offhanded way she then said something, I forget
what, about Ra*vel* and his Bo*le*ro. I understood immediately

that I had been corrected, but so gently that I took it only as a sign that she cared.

After she left Houston to marry Albert Erskine, we were out of touch for a while. I can't say exactly when I wrote her a long letter telling her all that I had been reading, thinking, and doing. She wrote back at once an even longer letter telling me what I *should* have been reading, thinking, and doing. That pretty much set the tone for the next forty years. She began to send me lists of books to read and music to listen to. Boxes of books began to arrive by parcel post. I was snatched a light-year's distance further along in my education and taste. A whole new world was illumined and revealed. It was my by-then-favorite aunt who did that for me, and I have never forgotten it.

Eleanor Clark said that Katherine Anne Porter had an intense but limited interest in music. I know exactly what she meant. Aunt Katherine refreshed and elated her soul with the music of Monteverdi, Purcell, Handel, Bach, Gluck, and Mozart, but had just a thin scattered interest in the composers who came after Mozart. More than anything else, she loved the songs and dances of the Middle Ages and the Renaissance. Often she would sing along, in a tuneless whisper, with her recordings of troubadour songs. She detested Wagner, and disliked most of the Romantics.

Naturally, there were exceptions. There are exceptions to just about anything you might say about her. For instance, she would listen to almost anything by anybody, if it was sung by Teyte, Baillie, Ferrier, or Pinza, or played by Hoffman or Lipatti. She knew by heart passages from the libretto for the Marschallin's role in *Der Rosenkavalier,* a character with whom she identified in ways. When we heard Lotte Lehmann's farewell performance in the role, she was disappointed that Lehmann wasn't wearing the golden wig she had worn in Salzburg years before. Nevertheless, she was touched to tears when the

Marschallin sang of the passing of time, of growing old, and of the death of love.

But you musn't think that classical music was the only kind she enjoyed. She would play "Stone Cold Dead in the Market" and "I May Be Crazy But I Ain't No Fool," laughing her head off every time. She thought Pearl Bailey and Fats Waller deliciously funny. She had recordings of flamenco, gamelan, and mariachi; Russian, Welsh, and Brazilian folk songs; Piaf, Mahalia Jackson, Trenet, and Dietrich. A friend once told her that her music, and I suppose by implication her taste, was like a bucket of water poured out on the floor, it had no shape. Her reaction was one of total astonishment, as if she couldn't believe her ears. Then she said, in an I'm-being-patient-but-watch-your-step tone of voice, "Angel, you are *wrong*, you know. Everything in my collection is *perfect of its kind.*"

Because of her lack of formal education, my aunt has been described in some quarters as uneducated. I don't understand this. Her library was superb. She was a voracious reader all her life, not just in and about world literature, but also history, biography, philosophy, psychology, religion, natural history, politics, art, music — just about everything except detective stories, which she described as the perfect way to kill time, for people who liked their time dead. She subscribed to dozens of magazines of every kind, from obscure literary magazines to *Southern Review* and *Hudson Review* to *Vogue, National Wildlife,* and *Cat Fancy.*

She read constantly, anywhere, at any time, always scribbling in the margins, underlining, and making notes. I remember that a friend called on the telephone, answered by my cousin Ann, and asked if Katherine Anne was busy. "Yes," Ann replied, "she is, she's busy correcting the *Encyclopaedia Britannica.*" She almost always read after retiring, letting the book sink to her breast as she fell asleep. If she awoke during the night, she simply raised the book, and went on reading where she had left off.

She loved poetry above all other forms of literature. I like poetry, but I can read it only in modest amounts. She read mountains of it, yards and yards of it, hours and hours of it, as easily and happily as I would read a favorite short story. She read it not only to herself, but aloud to anyone who would listen, and she read it beautifully, sometimes moving herself and the listener to tears. She read Eliot's *Four Quartets* to me from beginning to end. If I appeared baffled, as I often did, she would stop and we would discuss the passage. Other favorite poets, in no kind of order, were Homer, Dante, Shakespeare, the Goliards, Yeats, Crane, Warren, Marianne Moore, and many others. She also kept up with unknown and barely known young contemporary poets.

More than once she told me that she would make a bonfire of everything she had written if only she could be a truly great poet. She wasn't a good one, even; and of course she knew that.

She liked most animals, but reserved her special love for the felines: cheetahs, lions, tigers, jaguars, domestic cats of every breed and description, some of no known breed and beyond description. If she stayed in one place for any time at all, she always found a cat to coddle. She spoiled them outrageously, feeding them the same dishes she cooked for herself, allowing them absolute freedom with no discipline whatever. A superb Victorian sofa, the one praised in a poem by Marianne Moore, was sprayed by a gentleman cat named Juniper, bleaching the purple velvet with loops and squiggles like a Pollock painting. She was horrified when I suggested that Juniper be neutered, insisting that I had ruined the life of my poor Missy by having her spayed, no matter that Missy lived a happy eighteen years after the dirty deed. While I was in Texas on a visit, she stayed in my New York apartment to care for poor Missy. I had hardly landed in Houston before she called. Missy wouldn't eat; Missy wouldn't sleep; Missy wouldn't come to her; Missy hid from her; and every time she passed through the room, Missy hissed at her. "My God, darling," she moaned, "I have *never* been spat at by a small animal!" She thought I would have to return to New York at once; the situation was intolerable. The following morning I received a telegram: "DARLING: MISSY EATING LIKE A TRUCK DRIVER SLEEPING LIKE A BABY BEHAVING LIKE AN ANGEL STOP *WORRYING* AUNT KATHERINE."

If she ever owned a dog, she never mentioned it. She did say once that she wanted a bluetick Walker hound and a Tennessee walking horse, but I think that that was just her notion of what any Southern lady should have on the "property," which she also wanted and didn't have.

She was an early riser, I mean *really* early, and couldn't bear to have a visitor lying abed when she wanted his or her company. Around 5:30 A.M. she would call out, "Paul? Paul? Where are you, angel?" Surely she knew where I was; I was in bed. "Here," I would mumble. "*Where?*" in a rising tone. "Here," I would mumble again. "For God's sake, darling, *where! where!* Where *are* you?" In all my years in the Army, no barracks sergeant ever did a better job of routing me out of bed, wide awake and all attention.

It was important for me to be up because the choices for breakfast had to be discussed. At breakfast, lunch was planned. At lunch, dinner was arranged. At dinner, dinners of the past were remembered, and recipes detailed; and since everything reminded her of something else, there were always stories to be told.

Sherwood Anderson's wife, Elizabeth Anderson, visited Aunt Katherine in Mexico in the 1920s and wrote in her autobiography that she was a terrible cook. If that was true, my aunt pulled herself together and did something about it. She became absolutely first-rate in the kitchen, celebrated among friends and visitors for her table. She specialized in the French, Mexican, and Southern cuisines. That reminds me: I found in one of her cookbooks a recipe with which she had quarreled from first ingredient to last, scratching out this, adding that, altering something else. Finally, she scrawled a big *X* over the whole page and wrote in the margin, "No, no. As wrong as can be." I finally figured it out. She had tried, I'll never know why, to transform a recipe for chili con carne into a recipe for *mole poblano.* She almost did it, too, but not quite.

She collected dozens of cookbooks and bales of clipped recipes, and made more bales of notes. I believe she meant one day to write a cookbook, but never did. She was most proud of her Hellfire Sauce, which required seven kinds of hot peppers, and her homemade bread. She considered storebought bread fit only for feeding pigeons, and even that, she said, was cruelty to dumb animals. Until the age of eighty-seven she baked her own loaves and rolls, with every taste and texture imaginable.

She enrolled in the Cordon Bleu Cooking School in Paris, and bragged about her "thesis," an elaborate casserole that took her two days to make. She carried it home to her husband on the Métro, lifting the lid along the way so anyone who cared to could take a whiff. She took delight in imitating the sighs, kissed fingertips, and uprolled eyes of the whiffers.

She loved to cook, but hated the business of getting food from the kitchen onto plates. She quoted her maid in Paris, who remarked, "Madame, you are a cook most *formidable . . . mais! la présentation a manqué un peu!*" And certainly the process sometimes was "lacking." It would start with an alarming banging of pots and pans, the hiss and splutter of hot oil and the whoosh of flames, mingled with whoops, curses, and reassurances from Aunt Katherine that all was well. "Oh tweetlings," she would cry, "this is good, just you wait, you're going to like this!" And sure enough, she would emerge from the kitchen unscathed, triumphantly bringing with her some festive, fragrant dish.

I remember a dinner she prepared for Frank O'Connor and a young lady I believe was his wife. The main course was a leg of lamb, cooked according to a recipe given to Aunt Katherine by Ford Madox Ford. After the usual commotion in the kitchen, she brought out the lamb on a carving board and placed it on the table. She wouldn't allow anyone else to carve, and tackled the joint herself, slicing and hacking and talking a blue streak while the carving board tilted and slipped and gravy ran in little rivulets onto the table. We were all aghast, but after a moment realized there was nothing to do but relax and enjoy the skirmish taking place between Aunt Katherine and the lamb. She kept slicing and hacking and talking: "Samuel Johnson said that mutton should be carved in chunks, but I don't agree, do you? Anyway this isn't mutton, is it, we know that, don't we, this is a" — *wham!* — "tender little lamb." And that tender little lamb, once she had wrestled it into submission, was glorious. All things considered — the savory food, the vintage wines, and the lively talk — I'm sure that no one ever had less than a good time at her table.

Let me tell you just one more thing about Katherine Anne Porter and food. When she was a small girl she was taken backstage to meet the famous violinist, Maud Powell. Little Katherine Anne curtsied and told Powell that she was her idol; she wanted to grow up to be just like her. Powell hugged the child and told her that she must grow up to be like nobody but herself, and she must never have idols, they would only someday disappoint her. "And darling," swore Aunt Katherine, "I have never had an idol from that day to this." Charming, yes, but not quite true. She not only profoundly revered Joan of Arc and Erasmus, among others, but there exists a reference to one person specifically as an idol. "I hope," she wrote, "my idol Sir Thomas More forgives me for reminding us of this great final phrase summing up his life, his being." And what, you ask, does that have to do with food? Just this: I found those words in, of all places, her recipe for, of all things . . . egg custard!

It won't come as news to anyone who ever knew or met or just heard about Katherine Anne Porter that she was a great talker. Douglas Dick, then a young Hollywood actor, said that he could *hear* the punctuation when she spoke. I'm afraid, however, that I didn't enjoy her public appearances, least of all when she spoke extemporaneously, and she rarely spoke any other way, perhaps never did. I once asked her what she planned to say in a speech at the Poetry Center in New York. She replied that she hadn't the faintest idea, that she never knew what she was going to say until she heard it herself, and nobody was more surprised than she by what she said. Knowing this gave me such a fit of nerves that I could hardly stay through one of her performances, and I usually sat in the back row so I could slip out if I became embarrassed. Nobody else seemed to feel the way I did. There was always an air of anticipation, enthusiastic applause when she appeared, laughter at the right places, and at the end a standing ovation.

Naturally, I wasn't that apprehensive when she gave what you might call a private performance. One morning at Hay Meadows, the country residence of her old friends Monroe Wheeler and Glenway Wescott, the several house guests, hearing her voice, trooped one by one into her bedroom to say good morning. Her hair was tangled, she wore no makeup, and her eyes were puffy from sleep, or perhaps the lack of it. But she sat in bed propped up on pillows, sipping coffee brought to her by Monroe, a ratty old squirrel-skin cape draped over her shoulders by Glenway, and she talked. And talked. And talked. About Life. About her life. About her work. About friends and enemies. About cats. About coyotes, throwing her head back and imitating their howl. Gossip. Jokes. Poetry. It was dazzling, better than anything she had ever done in public, better than a lot of things I have paid money to see on Broadway. We were spellbound, we scarcely breathed. Nobody said a word. Finally, Monroe said that she must be exhausted, we had to leave, she really had to rest. "Oh my angels," Aunt Katherine cried, "I'm *not* tired, this has been heavenly. You *know* how I love good conversation."

Another time we were at a party given by Sidney Kingsley after an opening-night performance by Martha Graham and her dance company. To quote the old Ray Bourbon ditty, "We went to a party, and *everybody* was there!" I remember Helen Hayes, Eudora Welty, Martha Graham of course, famous actors and actresses, famous dancers, famous musicians and composers, famous people in packs and droves. Aunt Katherine made her way through the mob to a sofa and sat down, and in minutes she was surrounded by an audience, some of them literally at her feet. Surrounded, she sat there talking for the rest of the evening. In the cab afterwards, which we shared with Eudora Welty, Aunt Katherine chattered in a gay, excited way about the praise and attention she had received. Suddenly Eudora patted her on the knee and said gently, "Now Katherine Anne, don't be so girlish." My heart stopped. I waited for an explosion, but it never came. Aunt Katherine just laughed. She took Eudora's hand in hers, and said, "You're right, my darling; but it *was* a good party, wasn't it!" I wonder if anybody else in the world could have said what Eudora Welty said to Aunt Katherine and have had such an affectionate response. Perhaps, but I don't know who.

Aunt Katherine had very little sense of humor about herself, and you teased her at the risk of your life, or at least psychic maiming; but she had a great talent for fun. She could be difficult, unreasonable, touchy, often just plain impossible . . . but she was always fascinating, and more often than not, a joy to be with. There was the entertaining talk, of course, but also her warmth and her lively interest in just about everything under the sun. She generated a kind of infectious excitement which she imparted to those around her, making life seem more vivid, brighter, more completely *felt* than usual. Whatever she enjoyed, she enjoyed to the *n*th degree. She was reckless and fearless. There is a photograph of her at the age of seventy-something, perfectly coifed and smartly dressed right down to her high-heeled shoes, being hoisted onto a giant army tank by a squad of soldiers, held horizontal in the air above their heads like a rowing shell, a radiant smile on her face, without a flicker of concern about what anyone thought, or worry that she might be dropped on her head. You could almost call it a quintessential scene in the life of Katherine Anne Porter. In Bermuda, in her eighties, she decided that she was bored with wading in the ripples and wanted to go for a real swim, so off she went, headed for deep water, while Mrs. Hubbard, her nurse/housekeeper/companion, stood in the shallows clutching her skirts around her knees and screaming, "Stop her! stop her! stop her!" So a lifeguard promptly jumped into the water and swam out and stopped her. She was humiliated, furious. "That damned fool woman doesn't know how to have fun," she fumed, "and she won't let me have any!"

She loved jokes, bawdy ones included, which she told with great verve unless they called for obscenity. She simply could not say those words. Confronted by the big *F* she would press her lips together and go "mmph." "What?" I would ask, and she would go "mmph" again, and then say helplessly, "Oh angel, *you* know what I mean." She might just as well have taken that joke out behind the barn and shot it between the eyes.

After we saw the Broadway musical *A Funny Thing Happened on the Way to the Forum,* we exchanged silly lines from it for days. "I have terrible news," yelled one comedian. "I hope it is good!" yelled a second. Aunt Katherine said that the second comedian spoke for her, even after her long life of bitter disappointments, and she didn't suppose she would ever change. She said that on Judgment Day the Angel of Doom would probably thunder at her, "Katherine Anne Porter, I have terrible news!" and she would chirp, "Oh, I *hope* it is good!"

Porter at eighty-five, photographed by her nephew Paul Porter. Courtesy Paul Porter

We had our differences, Aunt Katherine and I, but now, re-membering her, I find that time has disposed of everything but the memory of her love, and warmth, and the pleasure of her company. Cousin Ann and I were talking on the telephone about Aunt Katherine several years after she died, and Ann suddenly burst out, "Dammit, Paul, I still miss her, I miss her all the time."

And so do I. I miss her more every passing day of my life.

Part Two

*Katherine Anne Porter and
the Transfiguring Imagination*

Problems of Personal Identity in Texas' "First Writer"

JOAN GIVNER

K̲ATHERINE ANNE PORTER tended to beat the drum a little when she spoke of her place in the literature of Texas, and the insistent message she beat out was this: *I am the first.* In 1975, she wrote the president of Howard Payne University:

> I happen to be the first native of Texas in its whole history to be a professional writer. . . . We have had . . . many people who wrote memoirs and saved many valuable stories and have written immensely interesting and valuable things about Texas; and they are to be valued and understood. But I am the first who ever was born to the practice of literature.[1]

Twenty years earlier she had told an interviewer:

> I am the first and only serious writer that Texas has produced. These young people may turn out to be first rate. The woods are swarming with writers. In all this ferment, we're bound to get more good ones. But so far I am the only one. If you can show me the others, I'll be glad to see them![2]

The young people she referred to were William Goyen and William Humphrey, and they would at that time have granted her the primacy she claimed. William Humphrey told her the same year that she was his sole teacher and that he wrote with "Old Mortality," "Noon Wine," "The Cracked Looking-Glass," and "The Old Order" open to his favorite passages. He admitted frankly that he stole his first published story from "A Day's Work." The fact that she was from Texas was especially important to him, since it had seemed to him beforehand that writers had to be from England, France, or New England, and he had thought his Texas origins spoiled his hopes.[3] And when he sent her a copy of *Home from the Hill,* Humphrey wrote in his inscription that she had taught him the greatest thing one writer could teach another: that the place and the life and the speech to which he was born were his place and his subject and his speech.[4]

Since Katherine Anne Porter was valued as a foremother by young men experiencing the anxieties of authorship as Texas writers, the question that naturally arises is: Who were the models and mentors who helped her with her own anxieties of authorship? After all, her claims of primacy are not exaggerated and she was indeed a trailblazer and pioneer, born female at the end of the nineteenth century and equipped with little formal education. She did have two heroines, although they were neither Texans nor writers. But they deserve attention because her devotion to them was so consistent throughout her life. They were Joan of Arc and Mary, Queen of Scots.

Her fascination with these two historical figures began very early in childhood when, a friend recalls, neighborhood children were instructed by Callie Porter to tie her up to the stake for a simulated burning.[5] And Katherine Anne Porter herself tells of a private game in which she created a miniature Joan of Arc from corn husks, tied her to a twig, made a funeral pyre, and set the whole thing alight. She intended the ritual as a gesture of homage, but her grandmother saw it as morbid, sacrilegious nonsense.[6] At a later stage, she also combined her interest in Mary, Queen of Scots with her love of performance.

When she was supporting herself by acting and singing on the Lyceum circuit in small Louisiana and Texas towns, she wore the costume of Mary Stuart, and one of her favorite pieces was the old ballad about waiting ladies of the queen, all called Mary.[7]

It is easy to understand the appeal of these characters for a young girl yearning for something beyond the usual scope of women of her time. They led such spectacular lives, with long imprisonments, bouts of activity, dramatic trials, and heroic deaths. Katherine Anne Porter often spoke of her early years, both in her fiction and in the fictions she created about her life, in images of imprisonment. Miranda Gay is "immured" in a convent,[8] and Katherine Anne Porter said that she married a man older than herself who "shut her up."[9]

But it wasn't simply with the historical personages that she identified. She came to her heroines not through the pages of the history books but through the great dramatic actresses who played them on the stage — Helena Modjeska and, in particular, Sarah Bernhardt, whose pithy sayings she always liked to quote. In published memoirs of her childhood, Katherine Anne Porter described her early experience of the theater:

> In those days all of the stars travelled in special trains or at least special cars gaily decorated, painted with their names on them. They travelled all over the country and they stopped at the smaller towns. I remember in my childhood I saw all the greatest actors and actresses, heard all the great pianists and violinists and singers in the world who came to the United States, because sooner or later they landed in San Antonio and El Paso.[10]

> Trainloads of audiences from all the small towns came in when Paderewski played . . . or Madame Modjeska appeared as Mary Stuart and who would have missed Sarah Bernhardt? I saw and heard all this when I was so young it was just a dazzling troubling dream, I knew nothing of it but the wonder. The wonder was enough. I would go dazed with my head a mere hive of honey-making bees for weeks, months, years. It unfitted me for living

as a simple child should, it tormented me with feelings and thoughts beyond my capacity, it urged me to strain against the bonds of childhood and the rules and the limitations, and the company of other children. [11]

That passionate response to theatrical experience is easy to understand because we know that Katherine Anne Porter had the makings of an actress — the dramatic skill, the imagination, the beauty, and what the critics call "star quality." When you see the movie *Ship of Fools,* or see the Hollywood portraits of her by George Platt Lynes, it is easy to imagine Katherine Anne Porter holding her own alongside Simone Signoret, Liz Ashley, and particularly alongside Vivien Leigh, whom she resembled in many ways.

Accidents of ill health and family problems turned Katherine Anne Porter's life in another direction. She went to Chicago when she was in her twenties with the full intention of being a film actress, but the work proved too strenuous. Yet, she acted in little theaters with great distinction for several years after that.

In "Old Mortality," young Miranda Gay is taken to see "a long sad play with Mary, Queen of Scots in it." She feels confused:

> Miranda thought the magnificent lady in black velvet was truly the Queen of Scots, and was pained to learn that the real Queen had died long ago, and not at all on the night that she, Miranda, had been present. [12]

Miranda fails to distinguish between the historical facts and people and the ritual of dramatic performance. Such confusion, one might add, is not all that uncommon. "Win one for the Gipper," former President Reagan used to tell his supporters, and Garry Wills describes Reagan's tendency to confuse his roles in war movies with war experiences that he never had. [13]

But for women of Katherine Anne Porter's time, the merging of artist and artifact, the creator and the work created, has a special significance. Two American critics, Sandra Gilbert and Susan Gubar, have explored this phenomenon in their monumental works, *The Madwoman in the Attic* and *No Man's Land,* and in numerous essays.[14] They have described the confusions of women writers when the pen was so closely identified with male generative power that for a woman to attempt authorship was often for her to feel unsexed, monstrous, and freakish. We know that women traditionally have been seen and have seen themselves not as creators of art but as works of art. They have adorned their bodies as works of art, decorated themselves, and been the subjects of paintings and songs, the muses of painters and poets. And they have been praised endlessly as works of art. "You are a poem," Ezra Pound told H. D., more taken with her than with her poetry.[15] Not surprisingly, women have functioned most comfortably in those arts in which the artist and the work of art fuse, where the physical body is the medium, as in the arts of dancing, singing, and acting. For this reason Katherine Anne Porter thought of acting, dancing, and singing when she dreamed of being an artist. Her physical beauty equipped her for the stage.

When she turned from acting to writing she did not abandon the habit of experiencing herself as a work of art. She often dressed for and acted out the parts of the characters she subsequently wrote about. In California, for example, when she was working on *Ship of Fools,* she wrote to Monroe Wheeler that she was writing to him while listening to Bach. She said she was dressed in her favorite white backless jersey dress, which had a wide canvas belt, and drinking a rum drink from a silver goblet.[16] The costume was that of Mary Treadwell.

A few years later she was in Ann Arbor doing a teaching stint. A student remembered:

> One day she came to our weekly meeting sporting a long string of pearls — down to the knees! Upon hearing us comment she went into a long explanation . . . saying she saw them in a shop win-

dow and when she knew they cost almost as much as she was making she decided to buy them.[17]

Just about that time she published the section of *Ship of Fools* in which La Condesa first appeared wearing her spectacular pearls.[18]

And when her work was finished, she performed it admirably. She was a huge success as a reader of her own stories, appearing in lovely evening dresses, preferably under a single spotlight. The imagining of her characters and their roles came as easily to her as did the reading of her stories.

It was the part between the two that caused difficulty—the actual writing down—and that was a slow and often painful process. Editors and publishers pleaded, coaxed, and used mild threats to get finished works. Marianne Moore called her the world's worst procrastinator.[19] I think that in part this difficulty came from the conflicts she experienced as a woman writer, between her sense of herself as creator and as a work of art. She struggled for an appropriate image of herself as writer and finally adopted that of pregnant woman. She spoke of her fertile writing periods as if they were confinements, involving visitation by a higher power, seclusion, a special diet, and final triumphant delivery.[20]

As I've suggested, one of the reasons that Katherine Anne Porter had difficulty was that her great beauty and elegant fragility made her seem more like a work of art than a working writer. Almost unconsciously, her eager fans, friends, and audiences—all of us—colluded with the image. More than one young man who came to learn from the writer fell in love with the woman and became her lover. When Dylan Thomas met her he held her to the ceiling in a drunken gesture of homage—but homage to what? Her art or her beauty? It is hard to imagine him holding up Dame Edith Sitwell or one of her brothers, all of whom he respected as artists. Karl Shapiro wrote a poem about the Dylan Thomas incident and included these lines:

> . . . everybody wondered what it meant
> To toast the lady with her own body
> Or to hold her to the light like a plucked flower.[21]

I think we have a pretty good idea what it means to do those things. The poetic tributes to her fall into the same pattern, quite different from those written to male artists. The poet-priest Raymond Roseliep wrote a number of poems to her, including these lines:

> The lady moves back and forth to her console
> the silver tea service, your cup, the throng of books. . . .
>   the lady. . . . (always the lady)
> who had mingled on deck with lovers and fools
> She rests her hands beside them,
> moonflower pale,
> light as a mussel shell.[22]

Those lines echo the portraits of ladies written by Ezra Pound or T. S. Eliot. Katherine Anne Porter was uneasy in her relationship with Raymond Roseliep. She said that his poems disturbed her, and she felt that she had let herself be edged, or nudged, into a false position.[23] The poems, like many of those written to her, were well-intentioned but sinister. As, when you think about it, was the title often attached to her: First Lady of American letters. "First Lady" is, after all, the title of a consort, a subsidiary position. If she is the First Lady, who is the President?

I've tried to suggest the extent to which the woman writer experiences herself as, in the words of W. S. Gilbert, "a singular anomaly." You may be thinking that all this is very well, but what does it have to do with the subject at hand — Katherine Anne Porter's relationship with her native state? Ambivalences in gender identity are rarely separate from racial, national, and regional identity. One has only to look at other women writers, such as Willa Cather and Gertrude Stein, to see how the conflicts in the women conflated with their attitudes to their

native places. Incidentally, Willa Cather provides many interesting points of comparison with Katherine Anne Porter. She
also claimed "firstness" in her native state, giving to one of her
fictional representatives Virgil's line "Primus ego in patriam
mecum . . . deducam Musas." When they shed their traditional female roles, they simultaneously distanced themselves
from their birthplaces. And so did Katherine Anne Porter.

When she left her first husband and abandoned the traditional role of domestic woman, she left Texas at the same time.
She returned, called back because her sister needed her, and
she remained in Texas because of ill health. When she resumed
a career in earnest, she again left Texas. Yet she was always trying to find ways of reconciling her past with the present, her
Texas experiences with her later experience, her female self
with her artist self. When she was farthest from Texas physically she was most present spiritually. She wrote "Noon Wine"
in Switzerland, "Old Mortality" in Paris, "The Fig Tree" in Bermuda. She may have finished these stories in the United States,
but they were hatched in other places. She said, "My time in
Mexico and Europe served me in a way I had not dreamed of.
. . . It gave me back my past and my own house and my own
people — the native land of my heart."[24]

Yet she craved a reconciliation that was more than spiritual.
In 1936, she traveled from France back to Texas and made the
journey to her mother's grave in Indian Creek. There she wrote
the poem that celebrates her homecoming:

> This time of year, this year of all years, brought
> The homeless one home again;
> Welcomed, homeless no more.[25]

Feeling reconciled to Texas, she returned in subsequent years
and lived for some months in Houston. But this attempt at
reconciliation ended in disappointment and rejection. The rejection culminated in 1939 when she was nominated for the
medal offered by the Texas Institute of Letters. Although her

book, *Pale Horse, Pale Rider,* included "Old Mortality" and "Noon Wine," the medal was awarded to J. Frank Dobie because of the indigenous nature of his subject matter and because of his long residence in the state. This pattern of attempted reconciliation repeated itself twice more at twenty-year intervals. The next time around she hoped to have a library named for her in Austin, but that hope was disappointed. About twenty years after that, she responded to the promises of the Howard Payne University in Brownwood to set up a room dedicated to her memory and filled with her memorabilia.

So far I have spoken of the part played in Katherine Anne Porter's attitude toward Texas by her own ambivalences as a woman. Now it is time to look at the other side of the question — how Texas feels about her as its first writer. She sensed, quite accurately, that her position had been usurped by J. Frank Dobie. It was to him that she referred when she spoke to the president of Howard Payne of the chroniclers and preservers of anecdotes and stories. In the interview I quoted at the beginning of this chapter, she also dismissed him as a mere chronicler. That reference was deleted by Ronnie Dugger, the editor of *The Texas Observer,* because at the time Dobie was languishing in hospital.[26] But chronicler or not, his ranch has been preserved as a literary shrine, a room has been dedicated to his memory in the Harry Ransom Humanities Research Center at the University of Texas at Austin, a university chair has been established in his name, and his papers and memorabilia are collected and cherished. There is, on the other hand, very little sign of Katherine Anne Porter at the research center, no picture of her on the wall, and if a journal wishes for a picture of her to accompany an article, there is precious little to choose from in the archive. It is as if she had never existed, and there is no sign that she spent her growing years just eleven miles up the road.

I have not been able to find out much about Dobie's opinion of Katherine Anne Porter. There is just a slight hint on the jacket of the biography of him by Lon Tinkle, who quotes his words: "I have sought the company of goat herders, lawyers with an eye for character and a zest for hunting, trail drivers and women who know how to cook frijoles in a black iron pot."[27] There's something about the conjunction of all those men of action and that greasy Joan keeling the pot that arouses my worse suspicions. And what I suspect is that Porter simply did not exist for Dobie. When in 1952 he revised his *Guide to Life and Literature of the Southwest* (first published in 1943), he had this to say about her:

> Katherine Anne Porter is as dedicated to artistic perfection as was A. E. Housman. . . . Her stories penetrate psychology . . . with rare finesse. Her small canvases sublimate the inner realities of men and women. She appeals only to cultivated tastes, and to some tastes no other fiction writer in America today is her peer in subtlety.[28]

Something about the conjunction of A. E. Housman and the repetition of "tastes" implies that Porter is not much to Dobie's taste. Elroy Bode wrote in *Alone: In the World: Looking:*

> ON KATHERINE ANNE PORTER: There seems to be a curious lack of breath and air in much of her work — a dry feeling, as if her words were too lacking in juices. There is no osmotic flow between the words and the experiences from which they were born. It is as though the stories were solely a product of her brain instead of that indefinable mixture of body and brain and spirit that apparently is the source of most good writers' creations. . . . When I do read her stories I find myself involved in a subdued and gentlemanly relationship: she remains there inside her book, contained within the carefully chosen words, and I remain in my chair — at a distance.
>
> Is it a lack of richness, of vitality, of verve that I seem to miss? Is it that I will grant her work the perfection of a Swiss watch — but then claim the right not to care too much for Swiss watches? . . .
>
> Sometimes it seems that in her strenuous effort to reach per-

fection of statement she squeezes the spark of life out of a story and all we have left are the carefully measured words. . . .

I will gladly walk past a Katherine Anne Porter exhibit in some museum of art — observing the small card which says, The Works of Master Story Teller. But I will not complain to the curator that the books are beyond my touch under glass — for that's where they have always been.[29]

You may think that Elroy Bode is not very important, but there are two things to note. One is that, although he dismisses Katherine Anne Porter, she was very much *there* in his early life. His mother was an important source for my biography because she attended the same school as Katherine Anne Porter in San Antonio and was a lifelong devotee of her work. The other rather interesting fact is that Bode's criticisms of Katherine Anne Porter are the same ones that are leveled at him — the small canvas, the sensibility, the prose style. I think that the influence of Katherine Anne Porter on Bode's work is greater than he wishes to admit. In that, he illustrates the point I am trying to make.

Larry McMurtry notes her presence, and he feels a need from time to time to demolish her as if he finds her a very threatening figure. His attack is frankly sexist. He finds her style "fragile, powdery and just plain boring." "The intensity of style conceals a small grain of experience." I think my biography has shown that few people had the variety and scope of experience that Katherine Anne Porter had of high life *and* low life throughout all the major centers of the Western world. McMurtry goes on to say that "a large part of her artistic experience is a high neurosis." But his final jab is that "there is nothing there" — that is, that she does not exist. "The plumage is beautiful," he says, "but after all, plumage is only feathers." He concludes, "Gertrude Stein, whom Miss Porter did not like, once made a famous remark about — I believe — Oakland, California. There was no there, there. I feel very much the same way about the fiction of Katherine Anne Porter."[30]

Not only does McMurtry want to erase her on his own account but also from the consciousness of other writers. When McMurtry turns to William Goyen he says, "Goyen went to school to the French, and worked hard to make his prose as elegant and firm as that of the French masters."[31] Now Goyen may well have gone to school to the French writers — don't we all? — but he also went to school to Katherine Anne Porter. As with William Humphrey, he acknowledged her importance in the copy he sent to her of his first book, which he inscribed in most flattering terms.[32] The letters exchanged between Katherine Anne Porter and Goyen during these years show that his inscription in the copy of *The House of Breath* was no empty gesture of homage.[33] Later the relationship between them became very complicated, and he had his own reasons for wishing to erase her from his record. Nevertheless, those early letters exist and prove the extent of her influence on him.

I think I have illustrated the common urge among Katherine Anne Porter's contemporaries, disciples, and followers to obliterate her from the record and to deny her preeminence as the first Texas writer to achieve national and international stature. The gesture, as you know, is not surprising, and it's not unique to Texas. It's one of the oldest games in the book — that of denying women primacy in creating anything from human life to works of art. And it is a gesture that Katherine Anne Porter understood very well indeed and recognized wherever she saw it, particularly in its earliest manifestation in the Book of Genesis. It was in a letter to William Goyen that she said the Adam and Eve story had always repelled her.[34]

Yet, for all the efforts to deny her primacy in Texas letters, Katherine Anne Porter will not disappear from the scene. Interest in her work continues to be high. Several excellent films have been made of her work in recent years, by a New York-based company in conjunction with a Dallas television station. Students in Canada, Britain, and China as well as in the

United States are working on theses, dissertations, and translations of her works. It may just be an accident, but I know of no student from Texas who is specializing in her works. Excellent books have continued to come out on her works in the last five years, but none by a Texas scholar.

And so, one might conclude that Porter's reputation is in good hands, and that her expressed wish "to be read and remembered" is being carried out. Yet, she didn't want to be a prophet without honor in her own country. She longed for reconciliation with her native state. When she died, her physical remains were brought back to Texas. One might expect to find something engraved on her headstone to mark her literary stature, such as "The first native of Texas in its whole history to be a professional writer" or perhaps "The first writer of Texas."

Instead, one finds the motto of Mary, Queen of Scots: In my end is my beginning. It is a motto that has a special relevance and resonance for Katherine Anne Porter.

As scholars have shown, when Katherine Anne Porter used a quotation it often proved to have many levels of significance. Mary's motto at first glance seems to refer to the religious beliefs she shared with Katherine Anne Porter and to the victory of the soul after death. But it was said also to have been the motto of her mother, Mary of Guise, whose emblem was a phoenix in flames with the words *En ma fin est mon commencement.* [35] (Katherine Anne Porter, you'll remember, was buried at the grave of *her* mother). Mary's motto points to the continuity between parent and child. The irony of Mary Stuart's life is that while she never reigned in England — never even belonged there, with her foreign connections and alien religion, and was indeed done away with by an English queen — her remains lie at the very heart and center of the English government system in Westminster Abbey. From her, every king or queen down to the present monarch is descended. (Nobody remembers or pays any attention to her husband, Lord Darnley.) It is Mary herself who, through thirteen generations, was the beginning. "I am the first," she might well say gloatingly.

It took twenty-five years for the rehabilitation of Joan of Arc after she had been burned at the stake. Katherine Anne Porter once wrote the introduction to a book on the retrial and rehabilitation of Saint Joan. Something about the cadences of her descriptions of the country people of Joan's region suggests that Katherine Anne Porter might have been thinking of, speaking of, the country people of her own region in Brown County and Hays County. She wrote:

> The people of Domremy knew exactly who Joan was, . . . each in turn tells us something about her, with great freshness of feeling and speech. Now that the Inquisition had lifted its ban, and they were free to say what they really thought, they claimed her for their own. When they said, "She was just like us," they meant to say also, "We are like her, she is one of the family, we never thought her so unusual, there were many others like her."

And she concluded:

> indeed what happened is so gently and Christianly true — she borrowed virtue from them, in turn. As they shed light on her childhood and young girlhood among them, by their love and remembrance saving her story for us, so she shed glory on them.[36]

It is high time the Inquisition lifted its ban on Katherine Anne Porter. I have attended several conferences that featured discussion of Porter and her works. Three were devoted exclusively to Katherine Anne Porter, one to the Texas literary tradition in which she figured only slightly, and one to the Texas women's literary tradition. There is an odd kind of segregation here. At the last conference Jane Marcus, casting a very cold eye on me, said that she hoped no one would try to crown Katherine Anne Porter queen of the conference.[37] I answered her then and subsequently in print.[38] I keep on repeating what I should like to see done. It seems infinitely reasonable, and usually everyone agrees. I would like to see a historical marker go up in Kyle to indicate that this is the town in which Katherine Anne Porter grew up. I should like to see her childhood home preserved and a marker placed on it and some mark in the cemetery where her grandparents are buried. I should like to see a picture of her placed in the Humanities Research Center and some effort made to acquire archival material that scholars could use. It is true that the chief repository of her papers is the University of Maryland, but she left a great deal of material, and there is still much that remains uncollected.

NOTES

1.   Joan Givner, *Katherine Anne Porter: A Life* (New York: Simon & Schuster, 1982), p. 44.

2.   "Miss Porter on Writers and Writing," interview by Winston Bode, *The Texas Observer,* October 31, 1958; reprinted in *Katherine Anne Porter: Conversations,* ed. Joan Givner (Jackson: University Press of Mississippi, 1987), pp. 30–38.

3.   Givner, *Katherine Anne Porter: A Life,* p. 374.

4.   William Humphrey, *Home from the Hill* (New York: Knopf, 1958), presentation copy in the McKeldin Library, University of Maryland.

5.   Erna Johns, interview with author in Austin, Texas, September 8, 1975.

6.   Undated fragment, McKeldin Library, University of Maryland.

7.   Givner, *Katherine Anne Porter: A Life,* p. 110.

8.   *The Collected Stories of Katherine Anne Porter* (New York: Harcourt, Brace & World, 1965), p. 193.

9.   Givner, *Katherine Anne Porter: A Life,* p. 86.

10.   Katherine Anne Porter, "Notes on the Texas I Remember," *Atlantic,* March 1975, p. 105.

11.   Katherine Anne Porter, "You Are What You Read," *Vogue,* October 1974, p. 252.

12.   *The Collected Stories of Katherine Anne Porter,* p. 179.

13.   Garry Wills, *Reagan's America: Innocents at Home* (New York: Doubleday, 1987), pp. 162, 171.

14.   Sandra M. Gilbert and Susan Gubar, *The Madwoman in the Attic* (New Haven: Yale University Press, 1979); *No Man's Land* (New Haven: Yale University Press, 1988); Susan Gubar, "'The Blank Page' and the Issues of

Female Creativity," in *The New Feminist Criticism: Essays on Women, Literature and Theory,* ed. Elaine Showalter (New York: Pantheon Books, 1985), pp. 292–313.

15. See Gubar, "'The Blank Page' and the Issues of Female Creativity."

16. Katherine Anne Porter to Monroe Wheeler, August 23, 1945, McKeldin Library, University of Maryland.

17. Richard Colewell to Joan Givner, February 8, 1971.

18. Katherine Anne Porter, "The Exile," *Harper's,* December 1950, p. 71.

19. Givner, *Katherine Anne Porter: A Life,* p. 164.

20. Givner, *Katherine Anne Porter: Conversations,* p. xvi.

21. Givner, *Katherine Anne Porter: A Life,* p. 368.

22. *A Roseliep Retrospective,* ed. David Dayton (Ithaca, N.Y.: Alembic Press, 1980), p. 76.

23. Katherine Anne Porter to David Locher, February 23, August 25, 1966.

24. *The Collected Essays and Occasional Writings of Katherine Anne Porter* (New York: Delacorte Press, 1970), p. 470.

25. Givner, *Katherine Anne Porter: A Life,* p. 295; Porter, *The Collected Essays,* p. 489.

26. Interview with Winston Bode, September 8, 1975.

27. Lon Tinkle, *An American Original: The Life of J. Frank Dobie* (Boston: Little, Brown, 1978).

28. See Lou Rodenberger, "Texas Women Writers and Their Work: No Longer 'Lady Business,'" *Texas Libraries,* 45 (4) (Winter 1984), p. 126.

29. Elroy Bode, *Alone: In the World: Looking* (El Paso: Texas Western Press, 1973), pp. 25, 26.

30. Larry McMurtry, "Ever a Bridegroom: Reflections on the Failure of Texas Literature," *The Texas Observer,* October 23, 1981, pp. 8–9.

31. McMurtry, "Ever a Bridegroom," p. 14.

32. William Goyen, *The House of Breath* (New York: Random House, 1950), presentation copy in McKeldin Library, University of Maryland.

33. Katherine Anne Porter to William Goyen, August 17, 1951, McKeldin Library, University of Maryland.

34. Porter to Goyen, August 17, 1951, McKeldin Library, University of Maryland.

35. Antonia Fraser, *Mary Queen of Scots* (London: Weidenfeld & Nicolson, 1969), p. 413.

36. Katherine Anne Porter, "Foreword," in Regine Pernoud, *The Retrial of Joan of Arc,* trans. J. M. Cohen (New York: Harcourt, Brace, 1955), pp. vi, vii.

37. "Texas Women's Literary Tradition: A Conference and Celebration," September 21 and 22, 1984, University of Texas at Austin.

38. Joan Givner, "Katherine Anne Porter: Queen of Texas Letters?" *Texas Libraries,* 45 (4) (Winter 1984), pp. 119–23.

A Southern Writer in Texas:
Porter and the Texas Literary Tradition

DON GRAHAM

UNLIKE MANY present-day Texas writers, Katherine Anne Porter was not embarrassed to be identified with Texas. She made the point explicitly in a 1943 letter to George Sessions Perry, in which she indicated it was acceptable to see her as a Southern, and more particularly a Texan, writer.[1] As usual with Porter, the admission was both precise and complex. I devote the next few pages to unraveling it.

Porter's letting herself be identified as Southern should come as no surprise to anybody. Since the late 1920s it has been an advantage for a writer to be identified with the South. For more than half a century now, the South has enjoyed a privileged status in American literature. From Faulkner to Welty, it never hurts among Yankee reviewers and academic critics to be called a Southern writer. Not only were there all those great writers coming out of the South, but also there was a significant body of Southern academic and professional critics—John Crowe Ransom, Allen Tate, Cleanth Brooks, Robert Penn Warren— who were shaping and defining modern literary criticism. Porter knew them all.

She was of course a great stylist, both in her writing and in the creation of her professional persona. In the script of her literary life she cast herself as a daughter of Southern plantation culture. She let close friends believe that the Miranda stories were gospel truth about a once grand Southern family fallen on hard times in the late Reconstruction South. She must have been a great actress. Until Joan Givner's biography appeared, many of Porter's close friends did not know that Porter's first marriage, which she at times conveniently forgot or reported had lasted only a brief time, in fact had lasted nine years. And one husband (it was her fourth, I believe) was married to her for a year before he discovered she was nearly fifty and almost twice as old as he was. In the literary marketplace, the role Porter played was that of an artistic Southern belle, a sort of Scarlett O'Hara who was also a literary genius. So there were distinct advantages to her in being identified as Southern.

To be called a Texas writer, however, was another thing altogether — and that is what is both surprising and refreshing about Porter's remark in 1943. At that time, being called a Texas writer was as bad as being called a Western writer. The label made people think of purple sage, Zane Grey, paperback racks in lonely bus stations in obscure fly-ridden towns, and cows and cowboys. The stigma of the Western label is just as strong today as it has ever been. The new *Columbia Literary History of the United States* — a pretentious and nearly worthless volume that sets out to redefine the boundaries of American literature and succeeds only in supplying jargon and ridiculous overestimates of minor writers — contains one mention of the modern Southwest, and of the West, it contains the following statements: "That leaves the West, which is really not a region in my context. It is all future and mobility — it is America."[2] What a strange remark! If the West is the most American place, or space, of all, why exclude its writers from consideration? The answer? "The Western writer perpetually confronts the impasse of the Western in literature, a formulaic convention assuming

the rigid identity of a popular literary genre dominating the
national mind and defining the whole space as either a book
or a movie."[3] Given such assumptions, only myopia can result.
Here are a few Western and Texas writers whose names do not
appear in the book: Wallace Stegner, Walter Van Tilburg
Clark, William Eastlake, Paul Horgan, Harvey Fergusson, Edward Abbey, Mary Austin (mentioned as a feminist but not as
a fiction writer), William Humphrey, William A. Owens, and
William Goyen. Porter of course is treated as a Southern writer,
so she is "safe." She escapes the Southwestern/Western taint, as
we are explicitly told: "Her emphasis on family relationships
and the insistent assertion of family history serve to Southern-
ize what would otherwise be a Western landscape."[4] I know
many Westerners who would be puzzled to learn that they are
not interested in family relationships and family history. The
most relevant corrective task I can think of in this connection
is Sallie Reynolds Matthews' *Interwoven,* a first-person narrative of family life in West Texas. But, returning to Porter, the
critic is almost right. Except that I would put it this way: in her
most personal Texas fiction — the Miranda stories — Porter has
raised her actual Southern background a couple of levels, up
to that of the faded aristocracy, and has deemphasized the
lower-middle-class, redneck facts of her actual upbringing.

In the 1930s, when Porter began to write about her Texas
past, she was by no means the first Texas writer to deal with the
Southern experience in Texas. And the period of her use of
Texas Southern materials — the mid-1930s through the 1940s —
corresponded to a flowering of Texas writing in the Southern
tradition. Porter, then, should be seen as a Texas writer in a
specifically Southern context. It is against this background of
what was happening in the literature of her region that I want
to set in relief the dimensions of Porter's likenesses to and differences from other, lesser writers.

This is not a study of influences; Porter probably did not
read the works of her contemporary Texas authors. Had she

done so, she would have found little of use. We know from her own comments that she was influenced by the best writing of the period—James Joyce, Gertrude Stein, Modernism. During her period in Corpus Christi, for example, in 1915 she discovered a copy of Stein's *Tender Buttons* in a local bookstore. Nothing in Texas literature even came close to such writing— not then, and not until Porter herself began to create in the 1920s, in stories set in Mexico, and then later, in stories set in Texas, a significant body of artistic work.

Among Porter's predecessors in Texas, Mollie Moore Davis deserves mention. Her *Under the Man-Fig* (1895) incorporated elements of East Texas folklore within a local-color format and told a convoluted tale of intrigue and race in a decaying plantation culture. Today only specialists know Davis's novel. In 1923, the year Porter's first short story appeared, fellow Texan Dorothy Scarborough published a novel dealing with cotton culture and featuring some scenes set in Waco. Scarborough, a folklorist, professor, and novelist, who held a Ph.D degree, is best known, of course, for her story of the harsh world of frontier West Texas, *The Wind,* published in 1925. In *In the Land of Cotton,* Scarborough memorialized cotton and condemned the risks, abuses, and injustices of its production. Only the large landowner prospers; only he has the resources to weather the shifting and abiding ills that afflict the raising of cotton. These include falling prices tied to unstable world demand, pestilential forces such as the boll weevil and the pink boll-worm, droughts, and floods. Scarborough also analyzes the paradoxical uses to which cotton can be put: as clothing, bandages, and other medical supplies, on the positive side; and, on the other, as wadding for ammunition and explosives. In World War I, the time when the novel takes place, cotton was invaluable on both counts. In Scarborough, as in most of the writers who dealt with King Cotton, the tendency to aestheticize the growing of cotton is strong. For Scarborough, the moment just before harvest is the most beautiful of all, and in this moment the South finds its fullest and most satisfying connection with the timeless agrarian impulse to sow and reap. A passage from *In the Land of Cotton* gives the flavor of Scarborough's lush romanticizing of a specifically Southern economic system:

> In autumn the fields are like other flower-gardens, each opened boll a great white chrysanthemum upheld on a five-pointed star. Level the fields stretch, vast, illimitable against the sky where rides the golden sun across his field of blue, where clouds hang fleecy as the cotton-wool. This is the time toward which the whole year turns, toward which the ardors of the wind, the cool assuagement of the dew and rain, the burgeoning beams of sun have gone. The cotton now is ready to be picked, for nature has done her part and perfect stands the yield. Man must do the rest. The air is mild and yet vast fields of snow stretch out and away. The year has passed with its wheeling changes, the elements have all been servitors for this. In such a white field one may trans-substantiate the furrowed winter, bare and gaunt, the mystic seed-time, the golden spears of light, the silver rain, the cruel heat, the drought of summer, the hopes and dreams and toil of myriad men. The heart of the south is visioned here.[5]

The passage reads as though Scarborough has rewritten Keats' "To Autumn" with cotton-picking as its subject.

Other writers within the Southern tradition made it explicit exactly whose task it was to express the heart of the South by harvesting the crops. A traveler to Texas in 1916, Tracy Hammond Lewis, knew he was in the South when he crossed the state line at Texarkana. Wrote Lewis: "There are three things that make the South different from any other place — cotton, coons, and caloric [heat]."[6] Such coarse racist formulations were not always absent from the fiction of the day, either. Laura Krey, writing in the wake of Margaret Mitchell's *Gone with the Wind* (1936), sought in her Texas novel of 1938, *And Tell of Time*, to give cotton culture an epic dimension. Set during the painful days of Reconstruction in Texas and based upon family memory and legend, *And Tell of Time* depicts a world in steep retrograde, the old order beset by alien forces — carpetbaggers and scalawags. In Krey's and other novels of cotton, the old order meant the perpetuation of a system of paternalistic enslavement even though slavery had been officially ended by the war that Southerners could neither forgive nor forget. Writing from inside the Confederate point of view, Krey sees in the planting season an image of immemorial certitude:

> Then, every year when the plowing was over, she would watch the negroes dropping gray, furry cotton seed into the pliant ground. Something in the scene, something in the warmer, ruddier light of April always reminded her, then, of the long sequence of aeons in which men had planted seed in rich soil, receiving it back, in due time, a hundred fold increased. And, as she watched the unhurried figures moving along the furrows, there would fall over her spirit the same deep calm that possessed her on clear winter evenings, when she caught a glimpse of black branches moving across a pale, opaline sky. Planting and growth, she told herself, sun and shadow, wind and rain, cold and warmth, had endured and would endure, regardless of any individual's brief pitiful life; and past, present, and future would always merge in a ritual of seed-time and harvest shared by all mankind. She wondered if men who lived in cities, cut off from the earth and its seasons, must not become, like fishes in dark caves, blind and directionless, swimming forever in circles toward some dimly remembered light.[7]

The viewpoint here is that of genteel observer, the overseer's overseer as it were. Those who do the actual labor, the "negroes," are transformed from workers into figures as peaceful and content as those on a Grecian urn; the act of labor becomes a pastoral moment, eternal and beautiful. Krey, who lived even longer than Porter, maintained the Confederate point of view into her mid-nineties. I know this because I talked with her in an Austin rest-home in 1982 or thereabouts.

The Southern cotton novelists in Texas wrapped their ideas about race in gauzy, cottony rhetoric derived from romantic

and pastoral traditions. Travel writers laid bare the superstruc-
ture of such views. Witness the words of one Nevin O. Winter,
in *Texas the Marvellous,* published in 1916:

> When the bolls have unfolded, and the pure white flow of the
> bursted pods greets the eye everywhere, the cotton fields of the
> Black Waxy Belt are a beautiful sight. In places they spread out
> almost as far as the vision reaches. Old white-haired negroes, look-
> ing like "Old Black Joe," and the comical little pickaninnies toil side
> by side all day long in the burning sun.[8]

To complete the literary background against which Porter's
evocation of Texas' Southern roots may be seen, I will mention
two more Texas works in the Southern tradition that represent
a big advance over Krey and Scarborough. One is George Sessions Perry's *Hold Autumn in Your Hand,* which appeared in 1941
and won the National Book Award, the first Texas novel to do
so. Perry's book is both a Steinbeckian document of the Depres-
sion years and a celebration of the courage and staying-power
of a white sharecropping family. Still readable and still in print,
Hold Autumn in Your Hand remains a vivid picture of cotton
culture as viewed from the bottom up, and not from the Krey-
Scarborough paternalistic stance from the top down. The last
novel I shall mention is the obscure *High John the Conqueror* by
John W. Wilson. The author's first and only novel, published
in 1948, it tells in a lean and effective style an incisive story of
the difficulties a black couple undergoes in living inside the
dangerous, segregated system of Jim Crow customs and an ex-
ploitative economic system of farm tenancy.

In the next two decades, the Southern tradition in Texas letters would find further and powerful literary expression in the
work of three writers, William Humphrey, William A. Owens,
and William Goyen. At least two of these, Humphrey and
Goyen, were strongly indebted to Porter's pioneering artistic
exploration of the Southernness of Texas culture.

Porter's use of Southern materials both paralleled and transcended the way in which her fellow Texas writers portrayed the South. For one thing, she made her part of Texas seem more lush, more redolent of the deep South than it might otherwise be envisioned. Her formative Texas years were spent in Kyle, in central Texas, sixteen miles south of Austin. The country-side looks western to somebody from East Texas, and it looks like East Texas to somebody from the Panhandle. (There are trees in Kyle.) Kyle partakes of both prairie and farmland, though it's mainly prairie. But when Porter describes Kyle, it's a place of honeyed heat and as luscious as anything in Thomas Wolfe or any of the other Southern lyricists. Let me break into a long catalogue of sensuous images from her essay "'Noon Wine': The Sources":

> heavy tomatoes dead ripe and warm with the midday sun, eaten there, at the vine; the delicious milky green corn, savory hot corn bread eaten with still-warm sweet milk; and the clinging brackish smell of the muddy little ponds where we caught and boiled craw-fish — in a discarded lard can — and ate them, then and there, we children, in the company of an old Negro who had once been my grandparents' slave, as I have told in another story.[9]

But even in such a rich description, one notes essential differences between Porter and her fellow Texas writers in the Southern tradition. Porter does not allegorize the landscape; she does not mythicize it into a Virgilian pastoral mode, nor does she politicize it to present, even covertly, the Confederate point of view.

It is precisely here, in her depiction of race, gender, and class, that Porter most completely distances herself from the provincial limitations of lesser writers, such as Scarborough and Krey. Porter understood better than any other Texas writer the complex interconnectedness of the races in the South, and the stories that bear upon this matter in *The Old Order* are a triumph of clear-headed, unsentimental humanity. Take the relationship of Sophia Jane and Nanny in "The Journey." As a child, Sophia Jane saw Nanny on the slave auction block. She called the black girl a "little monkey," and her father bought Nanny for her.[10] Between them, the two women bore twenty-four children "in the terrible race of procreation" (p. 334), and they became closer than sisters. Late in life, Sophia Jane is prepared to die first so that she can clear the way for Nanny to join her in heaven. And when Sophia Jane does die first, Nanny quietly but firmly renounces her lifelong service to Sophia Jane's children, grandchildren, and great-grandchildren, and takes up a separate residence, looking for all the world like some "aged Bantu woman of independent means" (p. 349). Just as quietly, Porter reveals the paternalistic economic basis on which Nanny's relationship with the family has always existed: she has been in continuous domestic service since childhood — during and after slavery, it is all the same — and it comes as a surprise to the heirs of Sophia Jane to discover how much labor Nanny ("Aunty") has contributed daily to their domestic comfort.

Nanny's husband, Uncle Jimbilly, from whom she also detaches herself — it was an arranged marriage, a matter of convenience, since both were slaves in the same household — is also treated unsentimentally. In "The Witness," we learn of his privileged position within the family. Bearing witness to the worst evils of slavery, Uncle Jimbilly narrates tales of horrible whippings and death incurred by slaves working on sugar plantations, but the stories are more moral exempla than felt experiences. Uncle Jimbilly himself seems to have survived slavery and the postslavery period very well. As the children amusingly realize among themselves, "since they had known him, he had never done a single thing that anyone told him to do" (p. 341).

In sum, *The Old Order* grants a common humanity to black and white alike, and avoids both the stereotype of "darkies" that characterizes the Confederate apologists and the other kind of stereotype that elevates blacks into pure victims or pure emblems of good. And in these stories, through compression, which is the essence of Porter's art, she is able to tell more about black-white connectedness in the South than have many volumes of fiction and nonfiction written from the most sympathetic viewpoint and with the best intentions.

As seen in the portraits of Sophia Jane and Nanny, racism in the South is also interwound with issues of gender. The Southern hierarchical view of social order imposed a heavy burden upon black and white alike. In her depiction of white Southern heroines in particular, Porter conducts a searching inquiry into the nature of gender and status in the South. Though nearly any of her Southern stories could be examined from this perspective, I will confine myself to the great short novel "Old Mortality" because it takes gender as its central theme. The novel explores three major roles for women. First there is the Southern belle, Amy, whose faded photograph and legendary status within a romanticized family history preoccupy the young sisters Miranda and Maria, posing an impossible ideal for them to try to achieve. As familiar in Southern lore as Scarlett O'Hara, Amy can be seen as Porter's antidote to Margaret Mitchell's sentimentalized heroine, just as the short novel, in a scant seventy-odd pages, virtually encapsulates the whole of Southern romantic history. Porter's great accomplishment is to grant Amy an interesting self-reflexive awareness of her predetermined role as Southern heroine. At one point Amy declares, "And if I am to be the heroine of this novel, why shouldn't I make the most of it?" (p. 189). And there are plenty of other hints that Amy knows full well the extent to which, rather than being the fairest flower of Southern society, she is instead an ornamental victim. Cousin Eva, the placard-carrying feminist, a woman who has been jailed for her political activism, offers a second and radically different feminine role. Eva hates the Southern belle tradition, the desperate measures to fit the codes of female beauty of that time and place — cinched waists, folk remedies to prevent the onset of the menstrual cycle. She denounces the cotillions and balls as a "market" where young girls fought to find men to marry; she says the whole thing "was just sex" (p. 216). But Eva is also at once embittered and romantic about the old order; a defect in Eva's looks kept her from being marriageable, and Miranda's dead mother, she tells her, was "a saint" (p. 217).

The third role, of course, is Miranda's. Here Porter brings to a close the sequence of Miranda stories that represent the greatest rendition of the initiation pattern in Texas writing. To be brief, Miranda, the engaging little girl who cannot hope to match the legend of Amy, considers several careers in this short novel. None of them are traditional feminine roles. At various times she wants to be a jockey, a tightrope walker and violinist (at the same time), and an airplane pilot. Her father makes fun of her at one point, saying she ought to be a lion-tamer. The point is that this true heir of the matriarchal power embodied in her grandmother Sophia Jane will have the strength to forge her own way in the twentieth century. Miranda is also in her own way a latter-day Amy—Miranda, after all, has eloped and married before she was eighteen, a signal act of romantic rebellion. Now she wants to be free to choose her own way in life; she wants to find out what life is by living it; she wants to *become*, not *be*. In the end, though the word is not used, she wants to become an artist. Like Joyce's Stephen Dedalus she will have to fly past the nets of family, religion, and province. What clinches the greatness of "Old Mortality" is the last sentence—and the last word in that sentence and story: "At least I can know the truth about what happens to me, she assured herself silently, making a promise to herself, in her hopefulness, her ignorance" (p. 221). This is in part what keeps the story from a too-easy optimism. Moving from the old order to the modern world, Porter knows, is not easy, but the act is necessary and indeed inevitable if Miranda is going to become, like Nanny, a "woman of independent means," an artist.

Besides race and gender, the third issue that separates Porter from the lesser writers is her treatment of class. If Southern society, in Texas or in Georgia, was about anything, it was about class—that is, social stratification based not upon ability or accomplishment but on birth, race, and sex. Virtually all of her stories in *The Old Order* explore the nuances and privileges of class, and the downward slippage that takes place in the status of Miranda's family is one of the ongoing concerns of the volume. But it is in connection with another of her Texas stories, "Noon Wine," that I wish to comment briefly upon the pressures of class in a stratified society. "Noon Wine" examines the economic and moral life of a white farmer and his family living on a small starve-out dairy farm near Buda, a tiny community a few miles north of Kyle. Royal Earl Thompson—and that first name is important—is at a low stratum of Southern society, but not the lowest. He is neither a poor white nor a Negro. In his self-deluding vision of himself as a man of property and leisure, he is a kind of parody of the plantation mentality. Through no act of his own, through the work of a strange man who wanders onto his farm and is employed by Mr. Thompson, the farm prospers, and Mr. Thompson actually comes to embody his dream-self of leisure, status, and power. Mr. Thompson's farm becomes a model for neighbors to admire. Then disaster strikes, the bounty-hunter comes, and Mr. Thompson murders him to avenge the Swede's presumed death and, more important, to save his own self-image, an image falsely based upon the labor and character of another person.

There follows one of the surest delineations of class structure in the history of Southern literature. After the trial is over and Mr. Thompson has been legally exonerated, he travels about the countryside in a direct appeal to his neighbors to try to prove to them, and to himself, that he is truly innocent of murder. His repeated journeyings lead him to try to explain his actions to "low-down white trash" families (p. 264). When they are unconvinced, when they hold a higher moral ground than Mr. Thompson, there is nothing left for him, not one shred of respectability or integrity.

Class, gender, race—in all three issues, Porter transcended

the limited perspectives of her time and place. At the same time, she remained absolutely faithful to the actual historical conditions of that time and place — pre–World War I central Texas, Southern to the core. And yet, at the very time Porter was lifting the very considerable body of Southern-based Texas writing to the highest level of art ever achieved by a Texas writer, within the state itself the Southern dimension was being erased in favor of the Western. The reasons were many, but three of them were J. Frank Dobie, Walter P. Webb, and Zane Grey. Although Dobie and Webb would not enjoy being linked with Zane Grey, in a true sense that is where they belong. Like Grey, they were interested only in the Texas of cowboys and *vaqueros,* of longhorns and unfenced prairies. In his 1937 opus *West of the Pecos,* Grey defined *real* Texas, which lay west of the "small part of Texas which adjoined Louisiana, and partook of its physical and traditional aspects. Now he wanted to find the real Texas — the Texas that had fallen at the Alamo and that in the end had conquered Santa Anna, and was now reaching north and west, an empire in the making."[11] The Alamo, Texas Rangers, and cowboys — those were the chief ingredients of the Texas myth that Grey, Dobie, Webb, and a thousand Western movies bought into and recycled until everybody from Alaska to Zimbabwe knew what Texas was: it was Southfork. The Texas of cotton farms, slavery, class structure, and the Confederacy was thus eclipsed by the Western myth. For too many years, Porter's Texas was obscured by both its similarity to the Deep South and its difference from the prevailing Western myth that sold so well in Texas. Now Porter's Texas is beginning to be better known. It is an act of historical recovery that still awaits its full recognition.

NOTES

1.   Katherine Anne Porter to George Sessions Perry, February 5, 1943, Humanities Research Center, University of Texas at Austin.

2. James M. Cox, "Regionalism: A Diminished Thing," in *The Columbia Literary History of the United States,* ed. Emory Elliott et al. (New York: Columbia University Press, 1988), p. 784.

3. Cox, "Regionalism," p. 784.

4. Cox, "Regionalism," p. 782.

5. Dorothy Scarborough, *In the Land of Cotton* (New York: Macmillan, 1936), pp. viii–ix. Originally published in 1923.

6. Tracy Hammond Lewis, *Along the Rio Grande* (New York: Lewis Publishing Company, 1916), p. 1.

7. Laura Krey, *And Tell of Time* (Boston: Houghton Mifflin, 1938), pp. 659–60.

8. Nevin O. Winter, *Texas the Marvellous* (Boston: Page, 1916), p. 218.

9. "'Noon Wine': The Sources," in *The Collected Essays and Occasional Writings of Katherine Anne Porter* (New York: Delacorte Press, 1970), p. 471.

10. *The Collected Stories of Katherine Anne Porter* (New York: Harcourt, Brace & World, 1965), p. 330. Subsequent references to Porter stories are from this edition, and pages are cited parenthetically in my text.

11. Zane Grey, *West of the Pecos* (New York: Pocket Books, 1976), p. 12. Originally published in 1937.

From Texas to Mexico to Texas

THOMAS F. WALSH

WHEN KATHERINE ANNE PORTER arrived in Mexico City on November 6, 1920, she had not yet written a single work included in her *Collected Stories,* published in 1965. Of the stories in that edition, more than two-thirds (70 percent) are set in Mexico or Texas. Mexico was not only the setting of her first story, "Maria Concepción," and her most famous story, "Flowering Judas," but also it triggered and sharpened her memories of her life in Texas. In "'Noon Wine': The Sources," Porter wrote, "So my time in Mexico and Europe served me in a way I had not dreamed of . . . it gave me back my past and my own house and my people — the native land of my heart."[1] "The Grave" perfectly illustrates her claim:

> One day she was picking her path among the puddles and crushed refuse of a market street in a strange city of a strange country, when without warning, plain and clear in its true colors as if she looked through a frame upon a scene that had not stirred nor changed since the moment it happened, the episode of that far-off day leaped from its burial place in her mind's eye.[2]

In this passage, Miranda, Porter's alter ego, recalls in a Mexican market an "episode" based on the author's own memory of her Texas childhood. I cannot prove but do not doubt that Porter records not only the seed of the story but the very circumstances of its appearance. This paper will explore other stories in which Porter's Mexican experiences recall or contain memories of her past, but it will first review her earliest and previously unknown Mexican writings because they reveal her attitudes toward life before entering Mexico and form a basis for examination of the theme of paradise lost in those stories.

Soon after her arrival in Mexico, Porter began to write for the English-language section of *El Heraldo de Mexico.* On December 15, 1920, she reviewed W. L. George's novel *Caliban.* The following is part of her conclusion:

> George sees plainly that the world is in a bad way, with nothing much to be done about it. He offers no remedy and indeed hints that there is none, for his conclusions are rooted in the profound pessimism of a thoughtful man who looks on a world in chaos, and hears the shrieking of a million Messiahs bent on setting it to rights each in his own way. . . . And out of it all the solitary victory that any of us can wring from life is the triumph of having achieved birth and the right to our day of sweat and confusion and half attained desires. Under the calm style you sense the hot revolt against an unendurable fact that must be faced out.

Even without the shift to the first person plural, this passage is a personal statement of the reviewer who goes beyond the ideas discovered in George's novel and formulates her own "profound pessimism" of the individual who achieves a "solitary" Pyrrhic "victory" by enduring the unendurable in "a world of chaos." The review reflects a deep-seated attitude that post–World War I disillusion does not entirely explain.

On December 13, 1920, Porter published "The Fiesta of Guadalupe," the first officially recognized work in her canon.[3] The opening sentence of the sketch firmly establishes its tone: "I followed the crowd of tired, burdened pilgrims, bowed under their loads of potteries and food and babies and baskets, their clothes dusty and their faces a little streaked with long-borne fatigue" (*Essays,* p. 394). The plodding sentence expresses the narrator's pity for the Indians' condition, their "long-borne fatigue" suggesting a permanent state of suffering. They have come to seek relief from the Virgin of Guadalupe, but the narrator indicates that their joyless pilgrimage is in vain. The sketch concludes:

> It is not Mary Guadalupe nor her son that touches me. It is Juan Diego I remember and his people I see, kneeling in scattered ranks on the flagged floor of their church, fixing their eyes on mystic, speechless things. It is their ragged hands I see, and their wounded hearts that I feel beating under their work-stained clothes like a great volcano under the earth and I think to myself, hopefully, that men do not live in a deathly dream forever. (p. 398)

The "hopefully" of the last clause does little to mitigate the effect of "deathly dream forever." Porter's passionate response to suffering here argues a predisposition to see what newspaper accounts of that day did not even mention.[4]

Porter's last significant contribution to *El Heraldo* was on December 17, 1920 — an account of the funeral of General Benjamín Hill, Mexico's minister of war. The last of two paragraphs reads:

> Life, full and careless and busy and full of curiosity, clamored around the slow moving metallic coffin mounted on the gun carriage. Death, for the most, takes his victories silently and secretly. And all the cacophony of music and drum and clatter of horses' hoofs and shouts of military orders was merely a pall of sound thrown over the immobile calm of that brown box proceeding up the life-filled streets. It sounded, somehow, like a shout of defiance in the face of our sure and inevitable end. But it was only a short dying in the air. Death, being certain of Himself, can afford to be quiet.

Here death, the pale rider, assumes an almost palpable presence. The "shout of defiance in the face of our sure and inevitable end" echoes "the hot revolt against an unendurable fact that must be faced out" in the George review, published two days before. The three *El Heraldo* pieces stress suffering, death, and fatalistic endurance — not the expected response of one who enthusiastically reported to her family on December 31, 1920, that she had attended the inauguration ceremonies of President Álvaro Obregón and hoped to participate in his new government with its utopian promise of land and liberty.[5]

"Xochimilco," based on a March, 1921, visit to that Indian village, is more in keeping with Porter's hope for Mexico's future.[6] The sketch pictures Indians in total harmony with nature: "They seem a natural and gracious part of the earth they live in such close communion with, entirely removed from contact with the artificial world." One Indian boatsman is an "independent human being vending his wares, under a kindly sky, in company with the poplars," while another "lives as a tree lives, rooted in earth, drinking in light and air." Porter, influenced by Christian and Precolumbian mythology, envisions Xochimilco as an Eden whose prelapsarian inhabitants are distinguished by their animal vivacity. Babies are "all friendly as chipmunks and as alert," while "placid children" play "without toys or invention as instinctively as little animals." Nathaniel Hawthorne depicted such an Eden in *The Marble Faun* through the person of Donatello, who is imagined as "enjoying the warm, sensuous, earthy side of nature; revelling in the merriment of woods and streams; living as four-footed kindred do — as mankind did in innocent childhood; before sin, sorrow, or mortality itself had ever been thought of!"[7]

Apparently, in "Xochimilco" Porter never thought of "sin, sorrow, or mortality," while in the *El Heraldo* pieces she thought of little else. It may not have occurred to her that some of the Xochimilcan Indians she admired were among those she had pitied at Guadalupe three months before. Nevertheless, "Xochimilco" is not an aberration from the rest of her works, for no American writer was more engrossed in the dream of

Eden. That dream led her into love affairs in which she idealized men as Miranda idealizes Adam in "Pale Horse, Pale Rider." It also caused her to lug her furniture — which she significantly calls, in "A House of My Own," "my personal equivalent of heaven and earth" — from "Mexico to Paris to New York to Louisiana and back to New York" in search of the place where she belonged. She failed to find it, however, because in her life "there was never permanency of any sort, except the permanency of hope" (*Essays,* p. 175). The perfect mate and the perfect house always eluded her. Only her hope remained "permanent," to be dashed over and over again. In "A House of My Own," she humorously describes the various calamities that befell her dream house in Saratoga Springs, adding in a wry footnote that she lived there "just thirteen months" (*Essays,* p. 179). But in most of her works hope remains to measure the depths of the despair her characters suffer. "Xochimilco" is unique only in its unqualified expression of the Edenic dream, but when it and the *El Heraldo* pieces are read together, they give the earliest published record of a lifelong conflict between hope and despair that began in childhood.

According to Joan Givner, when Porter read that the earliest impressions of childhood sometimes manifest themselves in obsessive fashion, she wrote, "So my horror and pain here and now from that old terrible time."[8] She was referring to her family's poverty, which contributed to the death of her mother shortly after the birth of her sister, Mary Alice, when Porter was two years old. Her father never recovered from his wife's death, blaming himself and his children for his loss and telling them that he wished they had never been born.[9] Porter wrote that "childhood is a terrible thing to remember. Wait till it reaches you in a flash."[10] In "The Grave," it did reach Porter in a flash. The horrible coupling of birth and death, in the form of the unborn rabbits Miranda and her brother Paul discover in the dead mother rabbit's womb, plays out Porter's guilt over her mother's death. The story abounds with images of a lost

Eden. The "pleasant small neglected garden of tangled rose bushes and ragged cedar trees and cypress" (*Stories,* p. 362) had become the family cemetery. Its recent sale makes Miranda and her brother feel "like trespassers" (*Stories,* p. 363), as if they had been expelled from Eden. But the empty graves in the neglected garden hold no terror for Miranda, who scratches around in them "aimlessly and pleasurably as any young animal" (*Stories,* p. 363), much like actual animals, "disorderly and unaccountably rude in their habits, but altogether natural" (*Stories,* p. 366). Also "simple and natural" is "the same outfit" (*Stories,* p. 364) of shirt, overalls, and sandals that the children wear. The outfit preserves their innocence by obscuring their sexual identities until "bad-tempered old crones" make Miranda feel "ashamed" (*Stories,* p. 365) of her boy's clothes, as Eve felt ashamed of her nakedness after breaking God's commandment. Up to this point Miranda had "faith in her father's judgment" (*Stories,* p. 365) in dressing them in such a practical (or innocent) manner, but only after the women speak does the gold ring found in the grave turn Miranda's "feelings against her overalls" and towards "the thinnest, most becoming dress she owned" (*Stories,* p. 365). Her sexual consciousness is stirred even more by her discovery of the baby rabbits, at which point the "very memory of her former ignorance" (*Stories,* p. 366) fades. After Paul hides the mother rabbit's body in the sagebrush, he warns Miranda to keep the secret of their knowledge, telling her, "Don't tell Dad because I'll get into trouble. He'll say I'm leading you into things you ought not to do" (*Stories,* p. 367). In this version of the Fall, Adam leads Eve into knowledge the Father had forbidden.

Although their images of Eden are similar, Hawthorne and Porter view the consequences of the Fall differently. Hawthorne suggests that Donatello's Edenic state was not fully human, whereas his fallen state has awakened his soul, "developing a thousand high capabilities, moral and intellectual, which we never should have dreamed of asking for, within the scanty compass of the Donatello whom we knew."[11] Porter offers no such version of *felix culpa.* Her characters often accept their fallen state, but surrender their Edenic dream with great reluctance. In "The Grave," Miranda buries her frightening knowledge in her memory until, twenty years later, it is dislodged—only to be buried again as she replaces it with the earlier memory of her brother Paul in his innocent state, "standing again in the blazing sunshine, again twelve years old, a pleased, sober smile in his eyes, turning the silver dove over and over in his hands" (*Stories,* p. 368).

Miranda's father in "The Grave" inadvertently attempts to preserve Miranda's innocence but leaves her vulnerable to the criticism of the "old crones" and unprepared to understand her sexuality. So Porter's own father had created in her the desperate need to cling to the innocence he ironically had denied her by plunging her into early guilt over her mother's death. That twinning of innocence and guilt is caught in "Baby," Miranda's nickname in "The Circus" and "The Fig Tree." Porter appropriated the nickname from her younger sister, Mary Alice, whose birth was more directly responsible for her mother's death, if any birth was. Thus the name "Baby" signifies both Miranda's desire to remain innocent and her father's desire to baby her, thereby leaving her unprepared to face the terrors of the fallen world. At the same time the name carries a guilt-laden reminder that a baby can cause its mother's death.

The three aforementioned Miranda stories, along with "He" and "The Downward Path to Wisdom," have as their theme the betrayal of innocents who are deprived of love and understanding, neglected, or imperiously ordered about in an atmosphere of repression. With "Virgin Violeta," the total number constitutes approximately a third of the *Collected Stories,* confirming Porter's own suspicions about her obsessions.

In "Virgin Violeta" (1924), her first published story about childhood,[12] Porter fleshed out what was apparently someone else's Mexican experience and invested it, consciously or not,

with her own emotional concerns so that it became a veiled version of her Texas childhood. The germ of the story came from
poet Salomón de la Selva's account of his seduction of the
daughter of a friend.[13] The story concerns a fifteen-year-old
girl's hysterical reaction to the advances of her poet-cousin
Carlos. At the same time Violeta strongly resembles Miranda
of "Old Mortality" (1938). In both stories, each girl is jealous
of her older sister, each is sexually innocent, each dreams of
becoming a raving beauty like her glamorous cousin but fears
that her dreams will not come true, each undergoes unhappy
experiences with a man, and each becomes disillusioned and
estranged from her family. Some passages in "Virgin Violeta"
seem to describe Miranda or her Aunt Amy perfectly. For example, "she wanted to wear red poppies in her hair and dance.
Life would always be gay, with no one about telling you that
almost everything you said and did was wrong. She would be
free to read poetry, too, and stories about love" (*Stories,* p. 24).
This passage reveals Violeta's total naïveté about life. Similar
to the children in "Xochimilco," she has "the silence and watch-
fulness of a young animal, but no native wisdom" (*Stories,* p. 23).
Carlos employs the same kind of image, telling her, "Ah, you're
so young, like a little newborn calf" (*Stories,* p. 29) — precisely
the quality that tempted him to seduce her in the first place.

The passage also stresses Violeta's desire to free herself from
the suffocating atmosphere her parents and the nuns of the
convent school create, attempting to deny or suppress all signs
of her intellectual and sexual maturation. Her father, seem-
ing even more remote than Porter's own father, prescribes the
punishment he expects her mother to carry out when Violeta
supposedly misbehaves. He warns Violeta, "It is your fault
without exception when Mamacita is annoyed with you. So be
careful" (*Stories,* p. 26). At school the nuns also stress careful-
ness, teaching "modesty, chastity, silence, obedience, with a little French and music and some arithmetic" (*Stories,* p. 23). At
home Violeta feels like a parrot stuffed in a cage, "gasping and

panting, waiting for someone to rescue" it. Church also "was a terrible, huge cage, but it seemed too small" (*Stories,* p. 26).

Violeta's ignorance of her sexual nature, which family and church conspire to perpetuate, results in her romantic fantasies of love and ultimately in her hysterical reaction to her cousin's unwelcomed kiss. The scene of his transgression is described as if it were a rape. When Carlos's mouth touches her lips, she "felt herself wrench and twist away as if a hand pushed her violently. And in that second his hand was over her mouth, soft and warm, and his eyes were staring at her, fearfully close. . . . Something was terribly wrong. Her heart pounded until she seemed about to smother" (*Stories,* pp. 28–29). This scene is charged with Porter's animus against de la Selva. As Carlos reads poetry to Violeta's sister Blanca, so de la Selva read to Porter every poem in a volume of Emily Dickinson's poetry. Carlos's poem about "the ghosts of nuns returning to the old square before their ruined convent, dancing in the moonlight with the shades of lovers forbidden them in life" (*Stories,* p. 24) is one de la Selva wrote after he and Porter had enacted what Violeta reads and dreams about. Porter also had an affair with de la Selva, whom she described as having "a sinister fascination that was not easily resisted."[14] And just as Violeta, at the end of the story, "amused herself making ugly caricatures of Carlos" (*Stories,* p. 32), so Porter draws an ugly caricature of de la Selva in "Virgin Violeta," which means, of course, "virgin violated." Both caricatures are acts of revenge, probably because Porter envisioned her affair with de la Selva as a violation and a reenactment of the first violation she suffered.

I am led to speculate about a first violation because the close kinship between Miranda and Violeta suggests a biographical source. Porter wrote no stories dealing with Miranda's adolescence probably because her own marriage occurred when she was approximately Violeta's age and was too painful to fictionalize directly. In "Old Mortality," Miranda refers to her early marriage only as "an illness that she might some day hope to recover from" (*Stories,* p. 213), while in "Holiday" the narrator speaks of being "too young for some of the troubles" (*Stories,* p. 407) she was having, prompting her to run away and recuperate from them at the Müller farm. In a letter to her father, Porter wrote that she was so terribly wronged in her first marriage that it took years for her to recover from it.[15] It is most likely that Porter, not as protected as Violeta but, like her, romantically inclined and sexually ignorant, responded to her husband's advances as if they were a violation from which she never quite recovered. Significantly, Porter also portrays threatened virgins in "The Dove of Chapacalco," written about 1922,[16] in "Maria Concepción," published in 1922, and in "Flowering Judas," based on experiences in 1921.

"Virgin Violeta" is a convincing re-creation of a male-dominated, repressively authoritarian alien culture, painfully similar in certain ways to Porter's own culture. Mexican convent schools must have reminded her of the fiction she once invented of escaping from a convent in San Antonio to marry.[17] In "Old Mortality," she repeated that fiction, Violeta's suffocating "cage" becoming a convent wall within which Miranda is "immured" (*Stories,* p. 193) and from which she escapes. When Porter considered resettling in the South, she wrote Caroline Gordon that she had left it because she was "simply smothered in the atmosphere of traditionalism and formalism, I ran away from it," adding that she had no intention of "not thinking what I please, nor of conforming where conformity would cramp and annoy me."[18] The "old crones" in "The Grave" and the judgmental neighbors of the Thompsons in "Noon Wine" and of the Whipples in "He" are examples of what would have annoyed her and threatened to curb her freedom.

In stories like "The Grave," Porter did return to Texas to recreate the familial conflicts that separated her from her roots. Her estrangement from her father caused her to portray her family's lost property as her first lost Eden, from which she was exiled. The image of the stranger recurs constantly in her works, but its significance was sharpened by her experiences in Mexico, where she was literally a foreigner with little knowledge of Spanish. "The Evening," written in 1924, gives us a mildly amusing picture of an American dancer surrounded by a group of Mexicans.[19] The woman, a *gringa fria,* wears a large hat shading her eyes in hope that it will make her look Mexican. She speaks "childish Spanish," but when her companions talk rapidly, "the language became a blur." "She could no longer understand the words, so she leaned back and closed her eyes, and the sounds translated themselves to her in terms of emotion." But a little later, she again "felt herself a foreigner, and the men at her table were strangers." "Holiday," also written in 1924,[20] is Porter's first story set in Texas, "in my south, in my loved and never-forgotten country" (*Stories,* p. 414), but the family the narrator visits there are German-speaking farmers. "Listening to a language nobody could understand except those of this small farming community," the narrator knows that she is in "a house of perpetual exile" (*Stories,* p. 413). Also enjoying the tranquil routine of farm life and the burgeoning of the Texas spring, extensively described in Edenic language, the narrator finds relief from her own troubles, but it disappears when she identifies with her double, Ottilie Müller. Crippled, mute, and excluded from the "tribal unity" of the family, Ottilie suffers and, more important, "she knew she suffered" (*Stories,* p. 426). For that distinct reason, "she was no stranger" (*Stories,* p. 426) to the narrator who is "a stranger and hopeless outsider" (*Stories,* p. 421) in the Müller household.

The ultimate story of cultural alienation is, of course, "Flowering Judas." A "*gringuita*" to Braggioni, Laura rejects "knowledge and kinship" with all, including her students, who "remain strangers to her" (*Stories,* p. 97). She goes on "errands into strange streets, to speak to the strange faces that will appear" (*Stories,* p. 101). Finding no pleasure in "remembering her life before she came" to Mexico, she cannot imagine living in "another country" (*Stories,* p. 93). She is indeed countryless, her estrangement reaching metaphysical proportions in that "she is not at home in the world" (*Stories,* p. 97). At the end of the story, she is like a ghost, attired in "a white linen nightgown" (*Stories,* p. 101), who dreams of Eugenio's invitation to leave "this strange house" and join him in a "new country" (*Stories,* p. 102) of death. The ghost image suggests estrangement in time as well as space, with Porter's characters returning to a place as if from the grave and discovering that they do not belong there. In "Holiday," Ottilie moved among her family "as invisible to their imaginations as a ghost" (*Stories,* p. 427). In "Noon Wine," Helton, "a stranger in a strange land" (*Stories,* p. 231), is like a "disembodied spirit" (*Stories,* p. 236), who speaks "as from the tomb" (*Stories,* p. 224). At the end of "Old Mortality," Miranda, alienated from her family, thinks, "It is I who have no place. . . . Where are my own people and my own time?" (*Stories,* p. 219). Like her dead Aunt Amy, whom she resembles in temperament, Miranda is a ghost just as her aunt was only "a ghost in a frame" to her.

"Flowering Judas" shows that Porter, feeling cut off from her own family and her Texas past, discovered in the foreign culture of Mexico total estrangement, just as she had discovered there perfect Edenic bliss.[21] Although she once described Mexico as her "familiar country" (*Essays,* p. 355)[22] her alter ego in "The Grave" moves, like Laura, through "a strange city of a strange country" (*Stories,* p. 367). And yet Porter clung to the "permanent hope" that she would find her place. That hope struggled against despair, fueling her imagination and shaping her fiction. Only there and in death could she return to her "loved and never-forgotten country."

NOTES

1. *The Collected Essays and Occasional Writings of Katherine Anne Porter* (New York: Delacorte Press, 1970), p. 470. Subsequent references to this edi-

tion, which includes "A House of My Own" and "The Fiesta of Guada-lupe," appear in my text.

2. *The Collected Stories of Katherine Anne Porter* (New York: Harcourt Brace and World, 1965), p. 367. Subsequent references to this edition appear in my text.

3. Porter included "The Fiesta of Guadalupe" in *The Collected Essays,* but incorrectly dated it 1923. The feast-day of the Virgin of Guadalupe is December 12. Since Porter's account of her visit to the basilica appeared on December 13, 1920, we can conclude that she wrote it overnight.

4. *El Heraldo*'s report of December 13, 1920, describes the religious cere-monies and the festivities outside the basilica, including cock-fighting. Al-though it briefly describes native dances, it makes no mention of Indian pilgrims, let alone their suffering, which is the subject of Porter's sketch.

5. Porter's letter is among her papers in the McKeldin Library of the University of Maryland. I thank staff members for their assistance in mak-ing them available to me. I also thank Isabel Bayley, literary trustee for Katherine Anne Porter, for permission to quote from unpublished Porter materials in this essay.

6. "Xochimilco" was published anonymously in *The Christian Science Monitor* on May 31, 1921 (p. 10). A fuller version, entitled "The Children of Xochitl," is among Porter's papers.

7. *The Marble Faun* (Cambridge, Mass.: The Riverside Press, 1888), p. 519.

8. Joan Givner, *Katherine Anne Porter: A Life* (New York: Simon and Schuster, 1982), p. 43.

9. Givner, *Katherine Anne Porter,* p. 48.

10. Ibid., p. 45.

11. *The Marble Faun,* p. 519.

12. "Virgin Violeta" was published in *Century* (December, 1924).

13. Enrique Hank Lopez, *Conversations with Katherine Anne Porter* (Bos-ton: Little, Brown, 1981), p. 83.

14. Ibid. Among Porter's papers is a fragment giving the circumstances of de la Selva's poem.

15. Katherine Anne Porter to her father, March 22, 1933, McKeldin Library, University of Maryland.

16. "The Dove of Chapacalco," never completed, is among Porter's papers, McKeldin Library, University of Maryland.

17. Givner, *Katherine Anne Porter,* p. 87.

18. Among Caroline Gordon's papers at Princeton University Library. I wish to thank the staff, for making the Gordon-Tate papers available to

me, and Isabel Bayley, for permission to quote. The letter is dated "January, Twelfth Night, 1931."

19.   "The Evening," never completed, is among Porter's papers, McKeldin Library, University of Maryland. I thank Isabel Bayley for permission to quote from it.

20.   Porter published "Holiday" in *Atlantic Monthly* in December, 1960. Dissatisfied with the ending, she had put it aside, to discover it among her papers many years later.

21.   The record of that one magical day in Xochimilco does not balance against the persistent images of estrangement in Porter's other Mexican works. Edenic images of her Texas childhood do not record the loss of something Porter once had, but, in retrospect, a promise of a life she never experienced. In that sense, all her Edens are strange lands.

22.   The phrase appears in "Why I Write about Mexico," a letter originally published in *Century* in 1923.

Estranging Texas:
Porter and the Distance from Home

JANIS P. STOUT

> *"It is I who have no place," thought Miranda. "Where are my own people and my own time?"* — "Old Mortality"

KATHERINE ANNE PORTER is not generally thought of as a regionalist. Though she was born in Central Texas and lived there, in the Austin–San Marcos area and then in San Antonio, Victoria, Lufkin, and Fort Worth until her mid-twenties, she is not identified with Texas in the way that Eudora Welty, say, is identified with Mississippi. To be sure, many of Porter's stories are set either in Texas or in some unspecified place in the rural South. Yet even in those stories that seem to draw most directly on her own childhood and family background — "Old Mortality" and the sequence known collectively as "The Old Order" — the sense of place is not compellingly Texan. It is possible for someone who has lived all her life in the state (myself, for example) and who ought to know Texas when she sees it to read Porter's stories and, unless the setting is very pointedly identified — as it is, for example, in "Noon Wine" — to imagine them to be set not in Texas but in some Southern region farther east.

In part, the "non-Texan" quality of Porter's work can be explained by reference to the multiregionalism of Texas and the Western conventions in which fiction and films presenting Texas are usually steeped. Don Graham explains that the state actually possesses at least two distinct regional characters — a Western aspect of ranching, cowboying, and the open range, and a Southern aspect of cotton growing, genteel manners, and a subordinate black class. It is the Western aspect that we are conditioned to expect. But Porter writes of Texas in its Southern aspect, and hence we do not readily see her as writing about Texas.[1]

Certainly Graham's comments, growing out of his unparalleled familiarity with the regional material whereof he speaks, are accurate as well as illuminating. Porter did write of a home region that she saw as more closely akin to the South than to the West. But that distinction alone does not account for the perspective that characterizes Porter's realization of place. It is not simply that her imagination was directed to a different subregional orientation than the one popularized in cowboy stories. For complex personal reasons, she needed to separate herself from her own childhood roots, even as she needed to draw on those roots for the generative power at the heart of her fiction. She does not so much choose one available version of Texas over another as shift and alter certain aspects of the place she remembered. In so doing, she distances *home.* And that act of distancing, of estrangement, is at the source of her detached fictive voice.

Most obviously, she distances herself from her Texas home by situating the greater part of her work elsewhere. Out of the twenty works that appear in the *Collected Stories* (twenty counting the "Old Order" stories as one, or twenty-six counting them individually), some thirteen are definitely placed outside Texas.[2] Two more, "He" and "The Jilting of Granny Weatherall," are indefinite, though surely Southern, in setting. Only four of the twenty *Collected Stories* (or ten of the twenty-six) are clearly set in Texas. And her only piece of long fiction, *Ship of Fools,* is set on an ocean liner bound for Germany.

In taking this roughly quantitative view, I do not mean to suggest that Porter should have restricted herself to Texas set-

tings. She was an unusually wide-ranging person, both geographically and experientially. It is entirely appropriate, and
indeed a tribute to her imaginative responsiveness, that she
could draw so successfully on varied scenes and social situations. Some of the stories set in Mexico are among her finest
works. In turning to Mexico, however, and to other settings,
she deliberately turned away from Texas. Yet if we select the
works that are commonly considered her best — "Old Mortality," "Noon Wine," the "Old Order" stories, "Pale Horse, Pale
Rider"—we can see that she seems to have achieved her finest
work when her imagination was turning backward, that is, to
childhood, to home.[3] And turning backward toward home and
childhood meant turning toward Texas.

Of course, a writer is not bound to inscribe the circumstances of personal experience. A homeward-yearning story
may be written with a focus other than that drawn directly from
autobiography. But Porter's narrative strategy, in the Miranda
stories at any rate, makes strong quasi-autobiographical claims.
Miranda bears such close resemblance to Porter herself—in
terms of year of birth (if we accept the year Porter often
claimed, which was not the correct one), family situation, and
personality—that we must take the character as a projection
of the creator. Therefore, by association, we take the rural
Southern settings in which Miranda grows up, which are in fact
labeled as *Texas,* as Porter's own growing-up place in Texas.
Born in Indian Creek, she lived in her grandmother's small
house in the town of Kyle, lying roughly thirteen miles southwest of Austin toward San Marcos, from 1892 until 1901, when
her father moved the family first to San Antonio and then to
Victoria. Yet even as she identifies certain of her fictional places
as her own region of Texas, she distances them from her actual
home by providing attributes that are not consistent with the
place or the conditions in which she spent her early years.

The act of distancing, of reshaping memories, is a complex
and significant aspect of Porter's imagination and a key to un-

derstanding her distinct fictive voice. Her relation to her home
state is problematic, biographically as well as critically. After
leaving Texas in her youth, she never again lived in the state
for any extended period. When she visited relatives in Houston, she was an exotic presence. Her nephew Paul recalls that
when he first met her at another aunt's house in Houston in
1936, when she was just back from Paris, she astonished the
family by appearing with rouged earlobes. They attributed her
outlandish mannerisms to her travels abroad.[4] In later life,
Porter often expressed nostalgia for her dear home in Texas,
yet she never chose to stay for long. Moreover, her interactions
with both family and such public groups as the Texas Institute
of Letters inevitably issued in misunderstandings.

Almost all of Porter's best work is set either in Mexico or in
a home place that is either explicitly or by resemblance Texas.[5]
But in numerous small ways, that home place is reconstituted
or resituated. It does not simply replicate the place where
Porter grew up.[6] Home is shifted eastward, so as to coincide
more nearly with the Old South. She sets up a pattern that is
repeated in less geographical ways as well, a pattern of the *unfamiliar familiar*. Thus, the home place is Texas, and yet it is not
Texas.

The ways in which Porter recreates or relocates her Texas
home are pervasive but at times so minor as to make the notic-
ing of them seem almost petty. In "Noon Wine," for example,
the setting is explicitly a "small South Texas farm" (p. 222). Because we know Porter began life on a small Texas farm, we as-
sume that the setting is near Kyle, as was the farm belonging
to Porter's grandmother, most of which was sold when the
grandmother moved into town, shortly before two-year-old
Katherine Anne (or more accurately, Callie) and her sisters and
brother came to live with her. In fact, the parallel is even closer
than that. The Thompson farm in "Noon Wine" is directly
modeled on the farm belonging to Gene Thompson and his
wife Ellen, who was a cousin of Harrison Porter, Katherine

Anne's father. The young Katherine Anne Porter lived with the Thompsons briefly while her father was again relocating.[7] The setting of "Noon Wine," then, is precisely placed in Central Texas near Kyle. Yet the Mr. Thompson of the story says that his previous hired men got in a fight "up the creek last week" and the survivor is now "in the hoosegow at Cold Springs" (p. 223). By today's map the town of Coldspring is more than a hundred miles to the east of Kyle, near the Louisiana border. Has another Cold Springs disappeared? Or is Porter simply exercising the novelist's prerogative of making up place names? Whatever the case, we notice that one of the speech patterns familiar to the untraveled Mr. Thompson is "Cajun," a dialect of Louisiana, which would not be near the Thompson farm if it is located where we think it is.

Neither of these details amounts to much. Even together they would be of little significance if there were not similar traces of an eastward pull in other stories that look toward home and therefore, given other close autobiographical parallels, toward Central or (as Porter specifies in "The Old Order," p. 332) "Southwest" Texas. We note that the grandmother in "The Old Order" objects to her new daughter-in-law as being "too Western" (p. 333). The grandmother's affiliations are more southeastern, befitting her Kentucky origins. In the story, as in Porter's own family history, the grandmother's generation was much more prosperous in its youth, in Kentucky, than in its maturity, in Texas.

In "Old Mortality," a work in which the backward look to childhood and to the dislocations of growing out of childhood is very strong, the sense of place in two of the three sections is surprisingly centered on New Orleans.[8] The legendary Amy not only goes to New Orleans on her honeymoon but speaks of doing so remarkably lightly, considering the distance — assuming "home" is where Porter's home really was. Actually, to maintain scrupulous plausibility the "home" of "Old Mortality" would need to be even farther south and west than Kyle, to make it possible for a person to ride horseback to the Mexican border and back in three days, as the story has it. Moreover, in her letter home Amy displays a surprising familiarity with New Orleans customs. Miranda and Maria, in the next and less prosperous generation, are sent to a convent school in New Orleans at late elementary-school age — an unusual choice for a Central or "Southwest" Texas family to make even if they were far better off than Porter's. The entire matter of the convent school would be much more believable for a family living two or three hundred miles *east* of Austin.[9]

We know that Porter did not go to school in New Orleans. Yet in developing her persona, Miranda, she chose in effect to push the childhood home eastward and to identify it, not consistently but strongly, with New Orleans. And just as her imaginative re-creation of home distances her actual home geographically by drawing away from Kyle and the Austin–San Marcos area toward the east, so she distances her early home qualitatively. Though she refers (in the "Old Order" stories) to the family's reduced circumstances, she makes the family much more prosperous than her own in fact was. Besides the costly recourse to out-of-state private schooling, there are circuses, concerts, balls, a two-story house with many rooms and a parlor mantelpiece with a Dresden-china figurine.[10] There is, specifically, a Mardi Gras costume ball to which Gabriel wears satin and ribbons and a wig while Amy goes in a specially made dress with basket skirts, white stockings, and green slippers, carrying a "gilded crook" (p. 185). One of the guests at the Mardi Gras ball is a "young Creole gentleman" (p. 186), who is evidently no stranger to the community since he had "two years before, been for a time engaged to Amy." Certainly Mardi Gras festivities can be held in any place, but the whole sequence is redolent of Louisiana and has a decidedly aristocratic cast. The Porters in fact lived like poor farmers, "cramped together in a tiny house," the children sometimes wearing "cast-off clothes" given to them by neighbors.[11] Certainly they did not have the extensive library—"sets of Dickens, Scott, Thackeray, Dr. Johnson's dictionary, the volumes of Pope and Milton and Dante and Shakespeare" (p. 324)—that is attributed to the Rheas in "The Old Order." Even in the generation before Katherine Anne's, which would have been the generation of Amy, the daughters would not likely have had velvet riding cloaks or the services of portrait painters.

Such inconsistencies with the facts of Porter's life are not to be regarded as blots, failures of verisimilitude. The world of Porter's fiction establishes itself in absolute integrity on its own terms. After all, she is not writing documentary, and the emotional tone is not dependent on the degree to which details of the story recapitulate biographical or geographical fact. That emotional tone, however, is very much tied up with the sense of home and with themes of belonging or not belonging. A feeling of nostalgia combined with resistance to the past, or of being at once bound and estranged, is pervasive in Porter's work. As Givner puts it, she "could not identify with her family and yet she craved a sense of identity."[12] Her ambivalent distance from home is a major ingredient in the detached yet affectionate narrative voice that so many readers have remarked on as one of the distinguishing characteristics of her style.[13]

The grandmother herself, in the "Old Order" stories, manifests the yearning for home which can never be satisfied because it is not identified with any fixed place. The central presence of Miranda's childhood (as her own grandmother, "Aunt Cat," was of Porter's early life), the grandmother provides the measure by which Miranda can assess herself and the world, but she provides also the standard that must be resisted if the child is to achieve autonomy. The grandmother is a principle of order and the embodied spirit of place and of familial belonging. Yet even she has led a disrupted life, being uprooted from her beloved home and insecurely resettled, not once, but in two successive removes. At the opening of "The Source," the first story of the "Old Order" group, we see both the grandmother's cen-

trality to the rhythms of the family's life and her powerful yearning toward home. Yet even at this stable matriarchal center
there is a duality to the homeward urge, a counterimpulse that
sets the pattern for Miranda's similar duality. In early summer
every year the grandmother begins to "long for the country"—
the farm where she lived before moving into town (p. 321). After
troublesome preparations disruptive to the entire family, she
arrives at the farm with "an indefinable sense of homecoming"
(p. 322). But after only a few days at the farm it would "come
over her powerfully" that she should be getting back, that the
house in town needed her. The whole process would then be
reversed, and she would "arrive at the place in town with the
same air of homecoming she had worn on her arrival in the
country" (p. 325).

Similarly, in "Old Mortality," Miranda and Maria feel exiled when they are sent away to school, and they yearn for
home, though they enjoy New Orleans on those rare occasions
when they are released from "immurement" at the convent. At
home, during holidays, their imaginations reach toward the
past. At the same time, they are compelled to resist the weight
and the distortions of the past, just as Miranda is later compelled to resist the pull of home by running away to get married. She needs to define herself against that powerful force
of family and tradition and to assert her individuality, yet at
the same time she needs the sense of belonging that she asso-
ciates with the past and home. At the age of eighteen, at the
end of "Old Mortality," returning home after her elopement to
attend Gabriel's funeral, Miranda concludes that she "can't live
in their world any longer" (p. 221). But its emotional hold on
her is evident throughout the closing section.

The ending of "The Grave," the last of the "Old Order"
stories, presents the converse to the ending of "Old Mortality."
An older Miranda who has distanced herself from home—she
is in Mexico, she is pursuing her own independent affairs—
looks back to childhood and Texas. Her vision of her brother

and the day they found treasures in any empty graveyard is a powerful vision of home, combining nostalgic longing with the newly awakened awareness of death. However, her estrangement is indicated not only by the faraway place where she finds herself but by the distant, self-absorbed expression she envisions on her brother's face. The yearning toward home remains with her—a continuing emotional closeness is implied by her seeing her brother so "clearly" (p. 368); but no overt emotional response to the abrupt remembering is indicated. She maintains her detached manner. The moment thus combines estrangement with homewardness.

In much the same way, Laura of "Flowering Judas" and the unnamed woman writer of "Hacienda" are estranged from home yet estranged also from those among whom they live. They are caught in dislocation. Laura finds herself in a strange land, caught up in events she does not understand and estranged, as well, from herself. Her dream of departure from the place of estrangement, which is simultaneously a kind of home—her own bedroom, a sanctuary in the midst of uncertainty and threat—is strongly tinged with forebodings of death.

The cluster of concepts of home/estrangement/death that we see in "The Grave" and in "Flowering Judas" appears also in "The Cracked Looking-Glass" and, more forcefully, in "Pale Horse, Pale Rider." In "The Cracked Looking-Glass," a story having no overt associations with Texas, we again find the same elements: a female character in a strange land, whose imagination continually turns backward toward her old home and who is misunderstood by those around her—that is, estranged. Rosaleen, the main character, comes from Ireland but is living in Connecticut. Claiming and perhaps believing that she has been called to her dying sister in a dream, she goes to Boston. In part the trip is an excuse for a lark, a chance to get away from her much older husband and the routine of their life. It is a little adventure, and she enjoys it. At the same time, the trip is an emblematic attempt to return home: by recovering her sister, Rosaleen will recover the familial past. The place where she expects to find her sister is not, of course, their true home in Ireland, but Boston, a place half-familiar, half-strange. And in fact the sister is not to be found even there. She has moved, leaving no forwarding address.

Disillusioned, hurt by her sister's neglect, and misunderstood, or perhaps understood too well, by a young Irish boy (someone from home) on whom she foolishly lavishes kindness, Rosaleen wants only "to be home and nowhere else" (p. 129). By "home" she now means her married home, not Ireland. But now her home is also, because of her husband's age and perceptible weakening, a place of impending death. The story ends with Rosaleen's fretful question to her husband, "If anything happened to you, whatever would become of me in this world?" and her querulous lament, "I could cry if you crooked a finger at me" (p. 134).

The most death-haunted of all is "Pale Horse, Pale Rider," another story with intertwined motifs of estrangement and yearning for home. The story begins with a sense of the unfamiliar familiar: lying asleep, Miranda feels that she is "in her bed, but not in the bed she had lain down in a few hours since, and the room was not the same but it was a room she had known somewhere" (p. 269). Her dream has taken her back to her early home in Texas, where her life was entwined with the lives of others in her family. In her dream she needs to "get up and go while they are all quiet." "They" are not the residents of the boardinghouse where she lay down, but her childhood family. Even her physical possessions are displaced from familiarity; they "have a will of their own in this place and hide where they like" (p. 269). Although "this place" might logically be the boardinghouse, where possessions would be hastily put away in temporary accommodations, it is apparently the place of the dream—home. The new place and the old are elided, and the old place, Miranda's childhood home, begins to seem less secure, less stable, than it once seemed.

In this first of several dreams, Miranda feels an urgency to get away before people wake up and begin to press questions on her. The intrusiveness of the family impels her to leave home even though she has "loved this house in the morning before we are all awake and tangled together like badly cast fishing lines" (p. 269). To assert her self, she must escape the entangling family by leaving home. Choosing a horse, one of the several whose names we recognize from the Miranda stories of the family past, she gallops away in the company of a thin, pale stranger. To make the essential step of leaving home is to start on a journey to death. This time, she pulls up her horse and lets the spectral stranger, Death, who is actually "no stranger" (p. 270) — he is a familiar visitor at home and joined her there, not somewhere on the road — ride on alone. But she knows she will go the distance with him another time.

Miranda's second dream, after she falls ill with flu, also involves vestiges of home, though home — Texas — is not specified. It is simply "another place she had known first and loved best," a place of "cedar, dark shadows and a sky that warmed without dazzling," "the spacious hovering of buzzards overhead" (a detail Porter mentions in "'Noon Wine': The Sources"), and a "broad tranquil river" (p. 299), plausibly the Brazos — again, a vision of home without the complication of people. But again that vision slides into death, a jungle of screams and threatening beasts and sulfurous rot, where voices cry out, "Danger, danger, danger," and "War, war, war" (p. 299). Once again the familiar shades into the unfamiliar, and nostalgia into fear.

Until hospital space can be found for Miranda, Adam, her doomed sweetheart, takes care of her in her room, and they talk about the past. Among the recollections they share is a song about death, "Pale horse, pale rider, done taken my lover away," which they had both heard in Texas, he in an oil field, she in a cotton field (p. 303). Again, home and death, nostalgia and resistance, are linked. As Miranda drifts into sleep, she dreams once more of death. This time it is a premonitory dream of

Adam's death, a premonition which will be fulfilled by the end of the story.

In the hospital, Miranda falls into a delirium in which sleep and waking, hallucination and reality, are mixed, so that it is hard to say whether she has several dreams or one long dream. In any event, her dreaming is dominated by death and undeserved suffering on a "road to death"—the journey she declined to take in the dream that began the story (p. 309). War, illness, and doctors come together with home in a scene in which Death, personified as a German soldier, throws poison into a "well that Miranda remembered in a pasture on her father's farm, a well once dry but now bubbling with living water" (p. 309). Home, the source of the redemptive water of life, becomes poisonous and arid as the "violated water sank back soundlessly into the earth."

In Miranda's last dream she passes through fears remembered from childhood into a phase of withdrawal from all awareness of bodily sensation or external attribute or any human concern. All that remains is the barest sense of individual being, a sense which melts into a vision of the afterlife. There, in an idyllic landscape, she recognizes "all the living she has known" and remembers "what relation she bore to them," but she feels none of the crowding and pressure that marred her actual memories of home. Family, home, are perfected—but they are perfected only in death.

In her best work, almost without exception, Porter combines estrangement with nostalgia and links the necessity of escape as an act of self-definition with the yearning for home as a symbol of secure identity. Both the distance and the yearning backward look are essential elements of her most authentic fictive voice—as they were of Porter's life. Leaving home early, absent for long periods, estranged from family yet doting on certain nieces and on her nephew Paul, she spent the greater part of her adult life searching for the ideal home and never finding it. Just as she moved from marriage to marriage, from lover to lover, so she moved from house to house — decorating, furnishing, planting, only to move again. Her personal possessions were apparently in storage more than they were in use. But she always wanted a home where she could have all her things with her and properly placed. It appears to have been her nephew Paul's arrangements for a large apartment (two apartments made into one) that led her to settle near the University of Maryland in her last years.

Porter's best work achieves a balance in this complex interplay of concepts of distance/autonomy and home/belonging. The lack of such a balance is at the heart of her failure in *Ship of Fools*. In this long novel, which was to have been her crowning achievement and which critics have at times wished to see as her final word,[14] every character is uprooted, estranged from home. Several of the major characters combine their estrangement with a yearning for a home known and loved in the past. But the effect of such yearning distance is not at all like the effect in Porter's short works because her own yearning is not implicated in her characters' nostalgia. The home for which most of the novel's characters yearn, Germany, is a place and a society Porter detested. The narrator's own distance from home, therefore, is absolute and unambiguous. It lacks the subtle complexity we sense in most of her work. Lacking that, the narrative voice is stilted and harsh. It is like a human face lacking the fine mesh of lines that give it character: such a face would be the face of a mannequin. Porter's voice in *Ship of Fools* lacks the humanity we hear in the voice, detached as it so often is, of most of her short works.

It is small wonder that readers of Porter's fiction, as well as of her life, have had difficulty assessing her attitude and relation to her home state. It is not simply a matter of region or state as geographic place, but of region as the totality of place and persons and social and economic condition. Porter's aspirations and need to define herself mandated her departure from a home that was dominated (in spirit, after her death) by a powerful matriarch who had herself left her home and come into a new land. Even as Porter's sense of self, we may conjecture, was modeled upon her domineering and repressive grandmother, her aesthetic affiliation was with that more complex "high" culture to which her grandmother also looked back. Her energy demanded that freedom from constraint which could not be hers in her familial home. If she occasionally falsified in her personal recollections and played fast and loose with facts in the geographic and economic attributes of fiction that gives every indication of being autobiographical, she nevertheless created in that fiction a precise delineation of the duality of her own yearning distance from home.

NOTES

1. See Don Graham, "A Southern Writer in Texas: Porter and the Texas Literary Tradition," in the present volume.

2. *The Collected Stories of Katherine Anne Porter* (New York: Harcourt, Brace and World, 1965). Subsequent citations of the stories appear in the text and refer to this edition.

3. "Pale Horse, Pale Rider," though set in Denver, turns insistently toward a rural home easily recognized as the Southern world of "Old Mortality" and similar stories.

4. Paul Porter, comments at a symposium held at Texas A&M University, April 23, 1988. See his memoir in this volume. Joan Givner refers to the occasion of this first meeting in *Katherine Anne Porter: A Life* (New York: Simon & Schuster, 1982), p. 294.

5. I am obviously begging the question of how we know what constitutes her best work. My judgment is that the generally recognized consensus in favor of "Old Mortality," "The Old Order," "Noon Wine," "Pale Horse, Pale Rider," "Flowering Judas," and perhaps three or four additional stories is correct.

6. Willene and George Hendrick put it summarily: "the biographical information she revealed was often romanticized or patently false." *Katherine Anne Porter,* rev. ed. (Boston: Twayne, 1988), p. 1. Givner (*Katherine Anne Porter*) gives considerable attention to Porter's dissimulation regarding her life.

7.   Hendrick and Hendrick, *Katherine Anne Porter,* pp. 67–69; Givner, *Katherine Anne Porter,* pp. 76–77. The Hendricks comment that in her essay "'Noon Wine': The Sources" Porter removes herself from the poverty-stricken scenes she recalls as the sources of the story by presenting them as scenes she observed. In fact, she actually lived on the farm where she observed them, and the story accurately reflects the condition in which she lived during her early years.

8.   The prominence of New Orleans in the story is an outgrowth of Porter's early fascination with her uncle Newell Porter's wife Ione, who in fact had eloped from a New Orleans convent to marry him (Givner, *Katherine Anne Porter,* pp. 57–58).

9.   Another detail that may seem improbable but in fact is quite accurate is the train by which an eighteen-year-old Miranda comes home at the end of "Old Mortality," traveling in a Pullman car. I am assured by Keith L. Bryant, an authority on business history and particularly on railroads, that such service was indeed available in 1912 on the Missouri–Kansas–Texas line southwestward from Dallas. What *is* implausible here, however, is the use of the word *village:* after alighting from the train they go off "down the rocky village street" (p. 218). A small town in Texas is not, and was not, a village. The word *village,* like Miranda's father's phrase, "graceful as sylphs" (p. 174), resounds with de-westernizing gentrification.

10.   The references to concerts and dramatic performances in "Old Mortality" (p. 179) are in fact plausible representations of events in Texas at that period, though it is not clear that they could have taken place in what Porter represents as the Rhea family's hometown or in the precise year of the story. Three of the five performers mentioned did play in Houston at least, and perhaps (or in the case of Paderewski, certainly) elsewhere. Sarah Bernhardt appeared in Houston on February 4, 1891; Helena Modjeska in Houston (in *Macbeth*) on January 6, 1898; and Ignace Paderewski in Houston and in San Antonio, but no other Texas city, in January, 1896. Indeed, in the mid-1890s there were playhouses in Waco, San Antonio, Fort Worth, Dallas, Austin, Paris, Tyler, Beaumont, Palestine, Columbus, and Brenham, as well as in Houston and Galveston, and perhaps elsewhere. See Joseph Gallegly, *Footlights on the Border: The Galveston and Houston Stage Before 1900* (The Hague: Mouton, 1962), pp. 157, 161, and 162. Porter's cousin Laredo Bunton, called Lady, enjoyed reminiscing about hearing a performance by Paderewski (Givner, *Katherine Anne Porter,* p. 57).

11.   Hendrick and Hendrick, *Katherine Anne Porter,* p. 3; Givner, *Katherine Anne Porter,* p. 46.

12.   Givner, *Katherine Anne Porter,* p. 77.

13.   For instance, Robert Penn Warren, in "Irony with a Center," notes her "air of detachment and contemplation." Originally published in the *Kenyon Review* in 1942 and included in Warren's *Selected Essays* (New York: Random House, 1958), the piece has often been reprinted. One convenient source is *Modern Critical Views: Katherine Anne Porter,* ed. Harold Bloom (New York: Chelsea House, 1986), pp. 7–21.

14.   In an early assessment, Harry John Mooney, Jr., wrote that *Ship of Fools* would "inevitably be approached as a kind of final statement, a summary of one artist's relation to the world around her" (*The Fiction and Criticism of Katherine Anne Porter,* rev. ed. [Pittsburgh: University of Pittsburgh Press, 1962], p. 61). That approach has not, in fact, been generally taken. As Mooney realized, such a view "raises troubling questions," and most readers have been inclined to regard the novel as considerably less important, and surely less perfectly achieved, than Porter's short fiction. Their view, I believe, is just. It is a disappointing book, and Mooney was correct in seeing that the "central limitation of the novel" is an error of the narrative distance (Mooney, *Fiction and Criticism,* p. 57).

Porter's Sources and Influences

DARLENE HARBOUR UNRUE

Those who admire Katherine Anne Porter's fiction and study it are aware that her own life experience was crucial to her art. Her childhood and adolescence in Texas are clearly apparent in such stories as "He," "The Jilting of Granny Weatherall," "Noon Wine," "The Old Order," "Old Mortality," "The Downward Path to Wisdom," and "Holiday." Her years in Mexico made possible the texture and topical themes of "Maria Concepción," "Virgin Violeta," "The Martyr," "Flowering Judas," "Hacienda," and "That Tree," and her Denver experience provided the context and the plot for "Pale Horse, Pale Rider." The New England and Greenwich Village years produced "The Cracked Looking-Glass," "A Day's Work," "Theft," and "Rope," and her first trip to Europe yielded "The Leaning Tower" and, ultimately, *Ship of Fools*. The relationship between the facts of Porter's life and the artistic rendering of the facts has been confirmed by the careful research of Joan Givner and others who over the years have contributed to establishing the correct biographical record. Porter herself addressed this relationship in her essays "'Noon Wine': The Sources" and "Why She Selected 'Flowering Judas,'" in which she recounted the events and impressions that fed into these stories.[1]

A considerable amount of scholarly effort has gone into attempts to locate Porter's "sources" beyond her personal experience. Porter unintentionally encouraged such forays by remarks she made. For example, she once declared that all her fiction was based on experience, either her own or someone else's that became hers on hearing it.² Sometimes she identified the other person's experience, as in "The Charmed Life," where she described an aged archaeologist in Mexico who told her the story of his foreman Juan and Juan's wife, Maria, a story that obviously became "Maria Concepción."³ It is also commonly known that "Virgin Violeta" was based on a story told to Porter by Salomón de la Selva, that "The Downward Path to Wisdom" was based on a childhood memory of Glenway Wescott, that the plot of "Magic" was told to Porter by a Greenwich Village maid who had worked on Basin Street in New Orleans, and that "The Cracked Looking-Glass" was based on a story she had heard in Connecticut.⁴ In fact, the germ of each of Porter's works can be identified as having emerged either from her personal experience or from the absorbed experience of other persons.

Because common sense tells us that experience borrowed can derive from a literary work as easily as from a secondhand anecdote, it has been tempting to look for the literary origins of Porter's fiction. The most likely sources are those writers and works Porter praised. She admitted to an admiration for Homer, Sophocles, Chaucer, Dante, Rabelais, Shakespeare, Sterne, Keats, Hawthorne, Melville, Twain, Tolstoy, Austen, Flaubert, Dostoevsky, Turgenev, Henry James, Eliot, Woolf, Yeats, Edith Sitwell, Joyce, Pound, Forster, Hemingway, and Katherine Mansfield, in addition to numerous others. Among their works she found special inspiration in Shakespeare's sonnets and *Cymbeline,* Forster's *A Passage to India,* Woolf's *To the Lighthouse,* Hemingway's *Big Two-Hearted River,* and Joyce's *Portrait of the Artist.* She said that Edith Sitwell's poetry had "range, variety, depth, fearlessness, the passion and elegance of great art,"[5] and she called Virginia Woolf "one of the glories of our time."[6] She placed herself among contemporary writers who were educated, as she said, "not at schools at all but by five writers: Henry James, James Joyce, W. B. Yeats, T. S. Eliot, and Ezra Pound."[7]

In spite of such a wealth of possibilities, however, efforts to prove the influence of particular writers on Porter's fiction have had limited success. The very first critical article on Porter, Lodwick Hartley's "Katherine Anne Porter," which appeared in the *Sewanee Review* in 1940, contains assertions that "The Ballad of Reading Gaol" inspired the conclusion to "Theft" and that "Noon Wine" leans heavily on Maupassant's "A Piece of String." Without arguing further for direct borrowing, Hartley also found in some of Porter's stories similarities to Steinbeck, Chekhov, and Woolf.[8] The best-known argument for a source is found in James William Johnson's "Another Look at Katherine Anne Porter," which appeared in the *Virginia Quarterly Review* in 1960. In that article, Johnson contends that the phrase "weep, weep" of "The Fig Tree" proves one of that story's sources to be Blake's "Songs of Innocence" and "Songs of Experience."[9] Although Porter knew Blake's work (she once agreed to write an essay on Blake for the *Yale Review*)[10] and although "The Fig Tree" depicts a state of innocence approaching experience, the argument is tenuous. Joan Givner's later suggestion that the sound came out of Porter's firsthand exposure to the tree frogs during her stay in Bermuda is more convincing.[11] Other source arguments have appeared steadily. In the same year as Johnson's article, Marjorie Ryan argued that some of Porter's stories are Joycean in technique as well as theme,[12] a comparison that has been made by others. In 1961 Joseph Wiesenfarth saw parallels between James's "The Beast in the Jungle" and "In the Cage" and Porter's "The Cracked Looking-Glass," in which he also found the influence of Joyce and Tennyson.[13] Givner associated *The Education of Henry Adams* with "Flowering Judas" and the Ugolino legend from Canto 33 of *The*

Inferno with "The Leaning Tower."[14] Rosemary Hennessy saw the Cinderella myth as the matrix of all the Miranda stories.[15] Most recently David Estes has claimed that "The Jilting of Granny Weatherall" contains explicit allusions to two poems by Emily Dickinson: "Because I could not stop for Death" and "I heard a Fly buzz—when I died."[16] In the best of cases, the assumption is sufficiently interesting or convincing to illuminate Porter's themes or techniques, but often the arguments are either strained or gratuitous. Porter openly declared that Sebastian Brant's fifteenth-century work *Das Narrenschiff* was the model for *Ship of Fools,* but she was quick to disparage critics' identification of specific sources in particular stories. From the time that critical books on her fiction began appearing in the late 1950s, she acquired copies of such books, and the margins are filled with her penciled-in reactions—usually indignant. For example, Porter made outraged disclaimers of Hendrick's suggestions that the source for the title of "Old Mortality" was Scott's novel of the same name and that the end of "Holiday" bore a significant resemblance to Frost's "Stopping by Woods on a Snowy Evening."[17] With only a few exceptions, the most successful source studies have been those that treat general influences, such as the Bible and myths, and those that stop short of insisting upon direct borrowing and instead argue merely for parallels and common ground.

All this is not to say that Porter was never inspired by another work or another writer or indeed that she never borrowed from them. There surely are echoes of Henry James, Austen, Flaubert, and Joyce, among others, in Porter's fiction. For example, the creation of the child Miranda in "The Circus," "The Fig Tree," "The Grave," and "Old Mortality" probably was inspired in part by the child characters of Henry James, as was Stephen in "The Downward Path to Wisdom." Porter, who admired finely drawn child characters, said that James' children were the best in all of fiction and praised his understanding of the child as a stranger in an adult world.[18] Many critics also have noted the similarity between Porter's style and Austen's, centered in their technical habits of placing rich meanings in restrained language. A strong case can also be made for the influence on Porter of Homer's *Odyssey* and Dante's *Divine Comedy*. Porter consistently named Homer and Dante among the greatest of artists. In "A Defense of Circe" (1954), Porter called the *Odyssey* "the most enchanting thing ever dreamed of in the human imagination."[19] In 1963 she told Caroline Gordon that she considered the *Odyssey* the "greatest single piece of literature in all history."[20] She wrote to Eugene Pressly in 1932 that she was working on "that book of Amy" (obviously "Old Mortality") and that she had named the second of its three parts "Midway of this Mortal Life," a translation of the first line from Dante's *Inferno*.[21] Her broad theme of rite of passage and her pervasive canonical metaphors of the journey and of descent into hell and ascent to enlightenment may well have been inspired by the *Odyssey* and *Divine Comedy*. However, the unavailability of definitive proof suggests that Porter assimilated her influences so perfectly, as Hartley observed early on, that even her literary sources became her personal experience.

Porter's assimilation of her sources made it possible for her to meet her own literary standards. She consistently described truth-telling as a literary technique rather than simply a moral standard, and she repeatedly praised careful craftsmanship. She said that her one aim was to tell a straight story and to give true testimony.[22] The agent of that aim was precise language that refused embellishment and contrivance. For Porter, the artist was not prophet, reformer, or politician. "It is not the artist's business," she wrote Bill Hale in 1932, "to divine the future, unless he has the faculty of divination and happens also to be an artist." Describing the artist as "sublimely superfluous," she said that artists' work is rediscovered when people want a "fuller record of the past" or when they want "light on the present predicament," but sometimes only when they want a work that is "fresh and beautiful and new."[23] She divided artists into two camps, which she called the James-minded people and the Whitman-minded people, and declared that she herself was firmly on the side of James. M. M. Liberman points out that in James, Porter obviously saw the triumph of "making"—the effective ordering of experience by means of style.[24]

When we consider Porter's collective statements about the value of art and the role of the artist, it is not surprising to hear her praising Katherine Mansfield for the magnificence of her "objective view of things" and "her genuinely first-rate equipment in the matter of the senses."[25] She praised Willa Cather for "her fine, pure direct prose";[26] Eleanor Clark for her "genius for attention, observation, and recording";[27] Max Beerbohm for his "excellent, disciplined way of writing";[28] Ford Madox Ford for his "craftsmanship";[29] and Virginia Woolf as a "born artist" and a "sober craftsman";[30] she praised Colette for being "such a good, sound, honest artist, a hard-working one."[31] Porter read many works other than fiction and many written by persons who never achieved greatness; what she cited as admirable in such works is a further witness to her aesthetic principles. Consider her review of *Daniel Boone: Wilderness Scout* by Edward White (1926). In it she says, "Daniel Boone, wilderness scout, comes alive without the prunes of moral or the prisms of hero-worship. The story has the virtues of clear writing, historical correctness and even of symbolic truth."[32] She found no place in art for hypocrisy, artifice, or propaganda. At the same time that she praised Willa Cather because she did not take up newness for its own sake, she expressed disgust for what she regarded as Gertrude Stein's self-conscious experimentation,[33] Christopher Sykes's overt message,[34] and the contrived effects of Edward Albee and Tennessee Williams.[35] She said of Ezra Pound, "He knew that art was no decoration, but the Stone itself."[36] The same aesthetic values she applied to literature she also applied to the other arts.

She had a lifelong admiration for primitive painting, calling children true primitives because of their honest view of life and their lack of self-consciousness in recording it.[37] But she made a serious distinction between true and artificial primitivism, and in the process she amplified her aesthetic values. In the letter to Bill Hale cited earlier she also wrote the following:

> I believe this rage for jazz, and for the so-called primitive in art, is a very evil sign. I remember from my earliest childhood the negroes dancing on the levee at New Orleans. The contortions and rhythms seemed strange to me but beautiful because the negroes really dance that way. I did not know, and I do not know yet, the secret of those harmonies which were so innocent . . . and completely right for those people and in that place. I can give a good imitation of the dances, I know all the steps and the music that goes with them, but the essential element is not in me, and my dancing is synthetic, like Diego Rivera's Indianism. . . . My sources are elsewhere, my imagination works otherwise, my very muscles have another kind of co-ordination. If I wish to amuse myself by imitating the negroes' way of dancing, that is all very well, for it gives me pleasure to experiment with that kind of dancing. But if I pretend to share their motives, their sources, that is merely dishonest, and very stupid dishonesty at that. Above all, it is corrupting to me, because I am being pretentious, and corrupting to the negro because it gives him false ideas about his motives which will end by leading him to sophisticate his own arts until they are ruined. . . . The modern civilized man has a hard road, but at least he made it himself, and must see it through on that basis. He must not turn back even to his own past for more than an occasional reference and orientation. If he runs for refuge to Africa, or India, or China, he is lost, because he then turns to a past that even these peoples have left behind them each at their own pace. And their pasts never existed for him by any descent close enough to make up the differences now. So all this jazz and children's art, and primitive painting, and return to Africa, and to Mexican Indians, and snobbish exaltation of ignorance and simplicity among our younger writers, is a sign of fatigue, of illness, a slackening of the whole system.[38]

Although Porter regarded conscious borrowing as dishonest, she could readily admit to inspiration, and she could safely use literary allusion. She resisted dogma as she abhorred slavish imitation. In reviewing two books by Kay Boyle in 1931, Porter listed a number of important American writers and observed that there was "not one but would have resented, and rightly, the notion of discipleship or of interdependence."[39] Porter's independence and her resistance to dogma grew out of her insistence on truth-telling. She finally said of Hardy, "In the end his work was the sum of his experience, he arrived at his particular true testimony; along the way, sometimes, many times, he wrote sublimely."[40] The same can surely be said about her.

Regardless of our difficulty in defining the influence of other writers on Porter, there is no doubt that she has had an effect on American letters, perhaps on world letters. As early as 1960, Johnson credited her with helping to launch the career of Eudora Welty; with turning the Freudian critical tide; with leading a revival of Henry James (still going on); with shattering the Gertrude Stein legend; and with holding artistic standards above politics in spearheading the awarding to Pound of the Bollingen Prize. Over the years a good many American writers — such as Flannery O'Connor, Tillie Olsen, and Truman Capote — claimed to have been influenced by Porter, but she professed not to see the proof. Margo Jefferson adds that, with Hemingway, Porter helped shape a peculiarly American language abstracted from regionalism.[41] We can add to their assessments only that Porter's high position in American letters is assured and that critical appreciation of her fiction has only increased. As the list of writers influenced by Porter continues to grow, perhaps we will be better able to describe her legacy.

She left behind a relatively small body of fiction that is exemplary in the harmony between its theme and its technique, a body of fiction so true to human experience and so profound that it yields new shades of meaning at every reading. It is as fresh today as it was when Porter wrote it, just as Homer and

Dante and Shakespeare and James remain fresh. In the decades and centuries to come, Porter's fiction no doubt will be examined under whatever critical light is current, and satisfied scholars will be convinced that they have discovered the "key" to Porter's fiction. Her real legacy exists in the technical perfection of her fiction and in the injunction to tell the truth, as it appears to the individual imagination. As much as she admired them, she warned against our being lulled into accepting the world as it is viewed by Homer or Sophocles or Dante or Chaucer or Shakespeare. The writers she has influenced will best use the influence by telling a straight story and giving true testimony.

NOTES

1. See *The Collected Essays and Occasional Writings of Katherine Anne Porter* (New York: Delacorte Press, 1970), pp. 467–82; and *This Is My Best,* ed. Whit Burnett (New York: Dial Press, 1941), pp. 539–40.

2. Barbara Thompson, "The Art of Fiction XXIX—Katherine Anne Porter: An Interview," *Paris Review,* 29 (1963), p. 103.

3. Porter, *Collected Essays,* pp. 426–30.

4. See Enrique Hank Lopez, *Conversations with Katherine Anne Porter: Refugee from Indian Creek* (Boston and Toronto: Little, Brown, 1981), p. 83; Joan Givner, *Katherine Anne Porter: A Life* (New York: Simon and Schuster, 1982), pp. 339–40, 197, 173.

5. "The Laughing Heat of the Sun," in *Collected Essays,* p. 63.

6. "Virginia Woolf," in *Collected Essays,* p. 70.

7. "It Is Hard to Stand in the Middle," in *Collected Essays,* p. 40.

8. See Lodwick Hartley, "Katherine Anne Porter," *Sewanee Review,* 48 (1940), pp. 206–216.

9. James William Johnson, "Another Look at Katherine Anne Porter," *Virginia Quarterly Review,* 36 (1960), pp. 598–613.

10. Darlene Harbour Unrue, *Truth and Vision in Katherine Anne Porter's Fiction* (Athens: University of Georgia Press, 1985), p. 227, n. 43.

11. Givner, *Katherine Anne Porter,* p. 212.

12. Marjorie Ryan, "*Dubliners* and the Stories of Katherine Anne Porter," *American Literature,* 31 (1960), pp. 464–73.

13. Joseph Wiesenfarth, "Illusion and Allusion: Reflections in 'The Cracked Looking-Glass'," *Four Quarters,* 12 (1962), pp. 30–37.

14. Givner, *Katherine Anne Porter,* pp. 218–19, 321.

15. Rosemary Hennessy, "Katherine Anne Porter's Model for Heroines," *Colorado Quarterly,* 25 (1977), pp. 301–315.

16. David C. Estes, "Granny Weatherall's Dying Moment: Katherine Anne Porter's Allusions to Emily Dickinson," *Studies in Short Fiction,* 22 (1985), pp. 437–42.

17. Givner, *Katherine Anne Porter,* pp. 465–66.

18. Unrue, *Truth and Vision,* p. 36.

19. In *Collected Essays,* p. 136.

20. Porter to Caroline Gordon, April 28, 1963, unpublished letter, McKeldin Library, University of Maryland. I am grateful to Isabel Bayley, Katherine Anne Porter's literary trustee, for permission to quote.

21. Porter to Eugene Pressly, November 18, 1932, unpublished letter, McKeldin Library, University of Maryland. I am grateful to Isabel Bayley for permission to quote.

22. See Hartley, "Katherine Anne Porter," p. 206.

23. Porter to Bill Hale, July 8, 1932, photocopy in the Beinecke Library, Yale University (my transcription). I thank Isabel Bayley for permission to quote.

24. See "Three Statements about Writing," in *Collected Essays,* pp. 451–52; and M. M. Liberman, "The Responsibility of the Novelist and the Critical Reception of *Ship of Fools,*" *Criticism,* 8 (1966), pp. 377–88.

25. "The Art of Katherine Mansfield," in *Collected Essays,* p. 50.

26. "Reflections on Willa Cather," in *Collected Essays,* p. 37.

27. "Eleanor Clark," in *Collected Essays,* p. 79.

28. "Max Beerbohm," in *Collected Essays,* p. 75.

29. "Homage to Ford Madox Ford," in *Collected Essays,* p. 249.

30. "Virginia Woolf," in *Collected Essays,* p. 71.

31. "A Most Lively Genius," *New York Times Book Review,* November 18, 1951, pp. 5, 52.

32. "History for Boy and Girl Scouts," *The New Republic,* November 10, 1926, p. 353.

33. See "Gertrude Stein: Three Views," in *Collected Essays,* pp. 251–83.

34. "On Christopher Sykes," in *Collected Essays,* pp. 64–67.

35. "Letters to a Nephew," in *Collected Essays,* p. 121.

36. "A Letter to the Editor of *The Saturday Review,*" *The Collected Essays,* p. 212.

37. "Children and Art," *Nation,* March 2, 1927, p. 234.

38.   Porter to Hale, July 8, 1932. Again, I thank Isabel Bayley, Porter's literary trustee, for permission to quote from this letter.

39.   "Example to the Young," *The New Republic,* April 22, 1931, p. 279.

40.   "On a Criticism of Thomas Hardy," in *Collected Essays,* p. 13.

41.   Margo Jefferson, "Self Made: Katherine Anne Porter," *Grand Street,* 2 (4) (Summer 1983), p. 153.

Part Three

"The Homeless One Home Again":
A Texas Bibliography of Katherine Anne Porter

"The Homeless One Home Again"

SALLY DEE WADE

Katherine Anne Porter spent most of her adult years vigorously denying a relationship with the state of Texas. She had unhappy memories of the state, she considered Texas a cultural wasteland, and she did not want to be associated in any way with the group of writers that Texas claimed as its own: J. Frank Dobie, Roy Bedichek, and Walter Prescott Webb. These writers were, from Porter's viewpoint, strictly regional, and the label "regionalist" held no attraction for her. She considered herself the only serious writer that Texas had produced, and in an interview in the *Texas Observer* she ardently disclaimed any regional association: "Of course I'm not a regional writer. . . . I don't know any first rate person who is a regional writer."[1]

A. C. Greene, former book critic for the *Dallas Times Herald,* however, found it strange that Porter was so vehement in renouncing her association with Texas because much of her best fiction has Texas as its background.[2] Indeed, many of Porter's short stories are built around Texas settings, Texans, and composites of experiences and memories from her childhood. Contrary to Porter's own comment, to identify Porter's work with a region is certainly no denigration of her literary talent. She used her background, experiences, observations, and imagination to create a fiction that reflects a region while it reveals truths that are universal. The regional aspect in her fiction provides richness, color, and depth of meaning without hampering the delicate probing of the human psyche. In all of Porter's work the regional issues are secondary to essential themes, but understanding her association with the area she fictionalizes is nevertheless important to achieving a more complete understanding of her art.

Porter's feelings for her home state were ambivalent. When she left Texas in 1914, she was trying to escape the pressures and unhappiness associated with her family and her marriage. For the next sixty-six years she attempted from time to time to re-establish ties with Texas; however, only in death did she find a permanent home in the state. Three factors particularly contributed to her attitudes toward Texas and Texans: her Texas family, those Texas writers associated with the Texas Institute of Letters, and her relationship with the University of Texas.

Much has been written about her relationships with the Porter family. Joan Givner, in her 1982 biography, *Katherine Anne Porter: A Life,* devotes ample space to the complexities of the family. To avoid redundancy, it should suffice here to say that the Porter family was composed of strong-willed individuals whose personalities continued to clash even after they left Kyle. Family arguments frequently erupted, particularly among the three sisters. With the exception of Gay Porter Holloway, Katherine Anne Porter considered her Texas family a group of quarreling illiterates. She indicated in a letter to Gay, August 8, 1949, that she felt a deep resentment and antagonism directed toward her by family members. Her pride in her almost total self-education coupled with her growing reputation as a writer developed in her an arrogance toward those she considered intellectually inferior, and that group included most of her family and most of another group: Texas writers and the Texas Institute of Letters.

The hostility that Porter felt toward Texas writers was apparent to a young writer from Texas, William Humphrey, who like Porter had chosen to live elsewhere. Porter befriended Humphrey in the early stages of his career when she was living in New York and he was at Bard College. Porter openly vented her hostility toward Texas when she told Humphrey in a letter of October 8, 1950, that she had willingly left the state early in her life and had no desire to return. She was always surprised to find another artist from Texas because she found it hard to believe that a state so culturally bankrupt could produce artists. Perhaps most revealing of her attitude toward Texas was her statement that only recently had Texas begun to recognize her ability as a writer and to include her in its group of writers.

The Texas Institute of Letters, founded in 1936, was composed of fifty members who wished to honor and promote Texas writers. The guiding force behind the Texas Institute was J. Frank Dobie, Texas folklorist, who saw in the camaraderie of the institute a "rallying ground for fertile talk."[3] He personally guided the institute and carefully screened all prospective members to ascertain if they met the qualifications of serious dedication to intellectual pursuits and a determined quest for truth-seeking in their writing.[4] The awarding of the institute's 1939 Book Award to Dobie over Porter's *Pale Horse, Pale Rider* set off a reaction that continued until 1964. In 1950, 1956, and 1964 the institute tried to woo Porter back to Texas to speak. In 1950, she first accepted the invitation, then turned it down, pleading illness. However, she later confided to her sister that she did not wish to share a program with Dobie.[5] In 1956, she again accepted then declined, this time because the institute could not meet her fees.[6] Finally in 1964 she accepted and arrived in Dallas, where she immediately contracted a respiratory ailment and had to be hospitalized.[7] It is little wonder that Larry McMurtry referred to her as "the Elizabeth Taylor of the lecture circuit."[8] She had no desire to be identified with a group who worshiped at the shrine of Dobie, Bedichek, and Webb. Mc-Murtry himself remarked, not quite accurately, that no one in the literary world outside of Texas has "heard of Bedichek, . . . read Webb," or was interested in Dobie.[9]

The final factor that contributed to Porter's attitude toward Texas involved the University of Texas. During the 1950s, Porter began to look back to her past for a sense of belonging. By that time, she was less interested in the past from a literary stand-point: most of her stories with Texas settings had been written. Instead, Porter needed to look back for her own sake. Despite the disparaging remarks she often made about the state, Texas once again began to attract her as she rummaged through her memories in search of a sense of home. In 1958, these memories, combined with a then-extravagant offer of $600 to speak, lured Porter home when the University of Texas invited her to participate in its Program in Criticism. Porter put aside all of the old grudges that she had against Texas and decided to make a triumphal return to her home state. It was to be her first trip to Texas since 1938, and she made elaborate plans for her presentation on the sources of "Noon Wine." She charmed her audience, and William Handy, a professor in the Depart-ment of English, wrote to her on October 31 that everyone from Dr. Ransom (then provost) to the undergraduate student body was most enthusiastic about her visit.[10] Porter was caught in the web of flattery, and her honeymoon relationship with Texas began. Unfortunately, the honeymoon did not last long, as a series of incidents quickly soured her enthusiasm for the state.

Porter's successful appearance at the University of Texas was noticed by Harry Ransom, who was in the process of establish-ing what has become one of the world's greatest collections of twentieth-century works, manuscripts, and private papers of American, English, and French writers. While Porter was in Austin, she was entertained at the home of a staff member of the university—probably Frank Lyell, since Porter mentioned in a letter to Frances Hudspeth that she had left a copy of the

Yale Review at his home.[11] During the course of the evening someone asked Porter what she planned to do with her literary collection, and she indicated that she might be interested in leaving her books, manuscripts, correspondence, and other papers to the University of Texas. Her statement was subsequently reported to Harry Ransom, and he purportedly said that the Katherine Anne Porter Collection was virtually assured.[12] Ransom wrote to Porter on November 7, 1958, informing her that the administration had voted to establish a Katherine Anne Porter Library in the Academic Center that was being planned for the Austin campus. In addition, Ransom invited Porter to return to the university in the fall semester of 1959 as a visiting professor.[13] Porter was enraptured; she loved nothing better than flattery and appreciation, and she was receiving both from the most unlikely source of all—Texas scholars. She decided that Texas would be the ideal place for her to settle permanently and wrote Ransom on November 16 that the Porter Library was the nicest memento of a life that she could imagine and that she looked forward to accepting the teaching position.[14] The long search for a home seemed to be over; Texas was the logical place to settle.

In her initial enthusiasm over the proposed Porter Library and the move to Texas, Porter offered her literary estate to the University of Texas as a token of her appreciation. In a letter of December 26, 1958, to Mody Boatright, chairman of the Department of English, she euphorically stated that she planned to give her entire collection to the University of Texas. She requested that he tell her exactly how and to whom she should offer the collection.[15] In an undated memo, Boatright requested Ransom to write Porter about her collection.[16]

On January 1, 1959, Porter wrote Harry Ransom requesting information on the new Porter Library, and she inquired what she was to do between the time of the announcement of the naming of the library and the laying of the cornerstone. Porter seems to have interpreted Ransom's letter and the university's

decision to name a library for her to mean that an entire building on the Austin campus would be named for her, but, according to Clarence Cline, a member of the Department of
English at that time, Ransom had intended merely to name a
collection within the Academic Center Undergraduate Library
for her.[17] Exactly when Ransom recognized the misunderstanding is uncertain, since there is no record of correspondence between Porter and Ransom clarifying the situation.

Meanwhile Porter accepted a Ford Foundation grant and
turned down the offer of the visiting professorship. Porter
planned to move to Texas during the time of her Ford Foundation grant, but she wrote to Boatright on August 9 that she
had decided to remain in Washington, D.C., because she
needed solitude for her work.[18] Actually, she had decided by
May, 1959, that she could not live in Texas. When she squarely
faced her decision to return, the unpleasant memories of her
youth came flooding back. In a letter of May 26, 1959, she told
her sister Gay that Texas was a strange land to her and always
would be.[19] The longer her absence from Texas, the more convinced she became that she could not live there and face the
unhappiness that she associated with the state.

The Porter Collection's permanent home remained in question. Porter had written to Ransom on June 16, 1959, alluding
to the interest that other universities had expressed in her collection. She raised the possibility of arranging to have a quali-
fied librarian help her with sorting her materials.[20] Ransom
reminded Porter in August, 1959, that the Porter Library was
acquiring outstanding pieces in Southern history and literature, and expressed the hope that she would agree to associate her work with the collection.[21] She did not respond to his
letter, but she began to suspect that her library would never be
built. She had written to her sister in May that she had no idea
when the cornerstone would be laid.[22]

In 1966 the question of the placing of the Porter Collection became a public issue. Porter announced that she was giving her papers to the University of Maryland. She had retrieved them from the Library of Congress and had decided upon Maryland as a suitable repository. The *Fort Worth Star-Telegram* and the *Houston Chronicle* ran articles stating that Porter was angry with the University of Texas and that she felt that Ransom had snubbed her. [23] The *Chronicle* quoted Porter as stating that she had written to Ransom repeatedly over the years about her collection but had not received a reply. The article then quoted Ransom as saying that the statement was not true: "I never had any communication with Miss Porter about this and I know nothing about it at all."[24] Porter subsequently wrote to Ransom attempting to explain the situation; she stated that she had never received an answer to her offer of her literary estate and that she was dismayed that anything promising so much happiness could have ended so badly. [25] Ransom immediately sought to clarify the misunderstanding by writing to her that he deeply regretted the incident, that he had received no direct word from her on the deposition of the collection, that the plan for the Katherine Anne Porter Library was still being carried out, and that he would never have ignored correspondence from her. [26]

One final incident in 1967 further strained relations between Porter and the University of Texas. Frank Wardlaw was director of the university's publishing division, the University of Texas Press. The press had a contract with Ronnie Dugger, editor of *The Texas Observer,* to publish *Three Men in Texas,* a collection of essays about J. Frank Dobie, Roy Bedichek, and Walter Prescott Webb. According to Wardlaw, Dugger and Porter had corresponded periodically since her visit to Texas in 1958, and Dugger requested her permission to use one of her letters to him in the book. A letter from Wardlaw to Porter of April 21, 1967, indicates that she had given permission. Suddenly Porter decided to rescind permission to use her letter and accused

Dugger and Wardlaw of playing dirty tricks on her. Wardlaw retorted that the press would remove the disputed passage, but he was disappointed in her actions.[27]

Katherine Anne Porter did not return to Texas until shortly before her death, when she attended a Homecoming Symposium at Howard Payne University.

NOTES

1. Winston Bode, "Miss Porter on Writers and Writing," *The Texas Observer,* October 31, 1958, p. 6.

2. A. C. Greene, *The 50 Best Books on Texas* (Dallas: Pressworks Publishing, 1982), p. 33.

3. William H. Vann, *The Texas Institute of Letters: 1936–1966* (Austin: Encino Press, 1967), p. v.

4. Ibid., pp. v–vi.

5. Porter to Gay Porter Holloway, October, 1956, McKeldin Library, University of Maryland.

6. Ibid., December 10, 1956, McKeldin Library, University of Maryland.

7. Lon Tinkle, "Spunk of KAP and Her Credo," *Dallas Morning News,* February 23, 1964.

8. Larry McMurtry, interview with author, Washington, D.C., June 8, 1982.

9. Larry McMurtry, *In a Narrow Grave: Essays on Texas* (Austin: Encino Press, 1968), p. 31.

10. William Handy to Porter, October 31, 1958, Porter Papers, Barker Texas History Center.

11. Porter to Frances Hudspeth, All Saints Eve, 1958, Porter Papers, Barker Texas History Center.

12. Clarence Cline, telephone conversation with author, October 18, 1982.

13. Harry Ransom to Porter, November 7, 1958, Porter Papers, McKeldin Library, University of Maryland, and Barker Texas History Center.

14. Porter to Harry Ransom, November 16, 1958, Porter Papers, McKeldin Library, University of Maryland, and Barker Texas History Center.

15. Porter to Mody Boatright, December 26, 1958, Porter Papers, McKeldin Library, University of Maryland, and Barker Texas History Center.

16. Mody Boatright, Memo to Harry Ransom, n.d., Barker Texas History Center.

17. Cline telephone conversation with author, October 18, 1982.

18. Porter to Mody Boatright, August 9, 1959, Porter Papers, McKeldin Library, University of Maryland, and Barker Texas History Center.

19. Porter to Gay Porter Holloway, 26 May 1959, Porter Papers, McKeldin Library, University of Maryland.

20. Porter to Harry Ransom, June 16, 1959, Porter Papers, McKeldin Library, University of Maryland, and Barker Texas History Center.

21. Harry Ransom to Porter, August 18, 1959, Porter Papers, McKeldin Library, University of Maryland, and Barker Texas History Center.

22. Porter to Gay Porter Holloway, May 26, 1959, Porter Papers, McKeldin Library, University of Maryland.

23. John Mott, "Novelist Irked at T.U.," *Fort Worth Star-Telegram,* December 18, 1966; "Writer Says UT's Ransom Snubbed Her," *Houston Chronicle,* December 18, 1966.

24. *Houston Chronicle,* December 18, 1966.

25. Porter to Harry Ransom, January 20, 1967, Porter Papers, Barker Texas History Center.

26. Harry Ransom to Porter, February 1, 1967, Porter Papers, Barker Texas History Center.

27. Frank Wardlaw to Porter, April 21, 1967, Porter Papers, Barker Texas History Center.

A Texas Bibliography of Katherine Anne Porter

T HE SELECTED Texas bibliography that follows, encompassing the years 1905–1987, documents the attitudes Porter held toward Texas, the views that Texas scholars have held about her and her work, and the attention she has received from the Texas media. It covers two of the three significant relationships that shaped her attitudes toward the state — those with Texas writers and with the University of Texas. Because of space limitations, the entire family correspondence cannot be listed. A summary of each entry is provided, with the exception of oral presentations. The bibliography is divided into several sections: (A) Porter's Work Published in Texas; (B) Articles about Porter Published in Texas Newspapers and Journals; (C) Theses, Dissertations, and Symposium Proceedings; (D) Books about Porter Published in Texas; (E) Porter's Correspondence with Texas Writers and the Texas Institute of Letters; and (F) Porter's Correspondence with the University of Texas. All of the entries up to the correspondence sections are in chronological order; correspondence sections are arranged in alphabetical order by the last name of the correspondent, and chronologically for each correspondent.

The following abbreviations are used throughout:

ALS   autographed letter, signed
CC   carbon copy
col.   column

corr.	correction
HW	handwritten
n. add.	no address
n. col.	no column
n.d.	no date
n.p.	no place of publication
n. pag.	no pagination
n. pub.	no publisher
n. sec.	no section
n. sig.	no signature
n. yr.	no year
p., pp.	page, pages
rev.	review
sec.	section
TL	typed letter
TLS	typed letter, signed
T. sig.	typed signature

Locations of collections of Porter material are abbreviated as follows:

KAP Papers, McL: Katherine Anne Porter Collection, McKeldin Library, University of Maryland, College Park, Maryland.

KAP Papers, HRC: Katherine Anne Porter Collection, Harry Ransom Humanities Research Center, University of Texas at Austin, Austin, Texas.

KAP Papers, BTHC: Katherine Anne Porter Correspondence, Harry Ransom Files, Barker Texas History Center, University of Texas at Austin, Austin, Texas.

A. Porter's Work Published in Texas

1917
   Porter, Katherine Anne. "The Week at the Theaters." *The Critic and Camp Bowie Texahoma Bugler,* 12 Jan. 1917, n. sec., n. pag., no. col.

Reviews four movies: *Until They Get Me, Empty Pockets, The Judgment House,* and *The Spirit of '17.*

1921

Porter, Katherine Anne. "Fashion's Follies: Let's Go Shopping with Marie; See What We Can See." *Fort Worth Record,* 4 Sept. 1921, n. sec., p. 2, col. 1–6.

Comments on the latest fashions and where to find them in Fort Worth; urges the women of Fort Worth to patronize the local merchants who have brought them the "best in style, quality and price."

Porter, Katherine Anne. "Fashion's Follies: Let's Go Shopping with Marie and See What We Can See." *Fort Worth Record,* 25 Sept. 1921, n. sec., p. 2, col. 2–4.

Comments on the fashions for fall, the length of skirts, styles of evening gowns, entrance of color into a woman's wardrobe; mentions the importance of being properly dressed.

Porter, Katherine Anne. "Fashion's Follies: Let's Go Shopping with Marie and See What We Can See." *Fort Worth Record,* 2 Oct. 1921, n. sec., p. 7, col. 3–5.

States that the autumn days demand new clothes; comments on the Lucerne apartment hotel and calls it the "meeting place of Fort Worth's best people who come together under their own roof and dance and play cards, or pass the hours in any kind of relaxation and pleasant and congenial surroundings."

Porter, Katherine Anne. "Fashion's Follies: Let's Go Shopping with Marie and See What We Can See." *Fort Worth Record,* 6 Nov. 1921, n. sec., n. pag., col. 3–5.

Comments on shopping in the Fort Worth area; mentions decorating for Christmas; suggests various gifts for friends at Christmas time.

1954

Peery, William Wallace, ed. *Texas Short Stories.* Austin: University of Texas Press, 1954.

Includes a reprint of "The Grave" (pp. 132–37), which had first appeared in *Virginia Quarterly Review,* 11 (1935).

1959
Porter, Katherine Anne. "Ship of Fools." *Texas Quarterly*, 2, no. 3 (1959), pp. 97–151.

Publishes a segment of *Ship of Fools* before publication of the novel; includes a literary biography in the "Contributors" section, p. iv.

B. ARTICLES ABOUT PORTER PUBLISHED IN TEXAS NEWSPAPERS AND JOURNALS

1. Newspaper Articles Published in Texas

1916
"What One Woman Is Doing to Help Children." *Dallas Morning News*, 10 Dec. 1916, Part 5, p. 7, col. 1–5.

Describes KAP's work with tubercular children at the Academy Oaks, Dallas County's first outdoor school. Mentions that KAP had been an instructor in elocution and folklore dancing in Corpus Christi. Describes the daily routine of the children and KAP's interest in them because of her bout with tuberculosis.

1935
A. C. "Unusual Short Stories by Katherine Anne Porter from Notable Collection." Rev. of *Flowering Judas, Other Stories,* by Katherine Anne Porter. *Dallas Morning News*, 1 Dec. 1935, Sec. III, p. 12, col. 4.

Reviews KAP's literary career; includes a brief summary of all of the stories; calls KAP a "little-schooled Texas woman, one of our most notable short-story stylists."

1944
Baker, Herschel. "Katherine Anne Porter's Art." Rev. of *The Leaning Tower,* by Katherine Anne Porter. *Dallas Morning News*, 1 Oct. 1944, Sec. III, p. 12, col. 1–2.

Calls KAP a writer's writer and places her in the literary company of Jane Austen, Rebecca West, and Ellen Glasgow. States that all Texans should regard stories like "Old Mortality" as the best fruits in regionalism because they have their source in KAP's childhood in Texas; comments that throughout the stories the prevailing mode, present in all tragic literature, is trying to redeem things that are gone forever; includes analysis of each story.

1945

"Katherine Anne Porter." *Dallas Morning News,* 5 Aug. 1945, Sec. IV, p. 4, n. col.

States that KAP is to be one of the first American authors to be published in liberated Europe; mentions that French, Italian, and Swedish editions of her work will be published.

1950

Tinkle, Lon. "Harper $10,000 Fiction Prize Again Is Selected by Distinguished Judges." *Dallas Morning News,* 19 Mar. 1950, Part III, p. 9, col. 4–5.

States that KAP served as a judge for the $10,000 fiction award given to *Debby* by Max Steele from Harper and Bros.

"Two Named as Winners of Awards." *Dallas Morning News,* Early City Ed., 13 Nov. 1950, Part II, p. 6, col. 3.

Names KAP and J. Frank Dobie as recipients of the first annual A. Harris & Company Texas Award at the Texas Institute of Letters; describes the award as honoring achievement by outstanding Texans who have made significant contributions to America in the arts and sciences.

1951

Leslie, Warren. "The Art of Katherine Anne Porter." *Dallas Morning News,* 7 Jan. 1951, Sec. IV, p. 6, col. 6–8.

Comments about KAP's writing; includes a brief analysis of "The Leaning Tower," "Pale Horse, Pale Rider," "Old Mortality," and "Noon Wine"; states that KAP has leanness and economy in her writing that unite with imagination to create a memorable fiction.

1952

Fuermann, George. "Post Card." *Houston Post,* 6 Oct. 1952, Sec. 2, p. 6, n. col.

Mentions Mrs. Gay Porter Holloway, to whom *The Days Before,* by KAP, was dedicated.

Taylor, Norris. "Art, Not Artifice, Is Key to Porter Writing." Rev. of *The Days Before* by Katherine Anne Porter. *Houston Post,* 26 Oct. 1952, Sec. 7, p. 7, col. 2–3.

States that KAP's prose is "one phrase pulling another like a linked chain, the whole not to be unstrung from any of the parts." Compliments KAP's perceptive insight into the life and work of Henry James and says that her short piece about James does as much to reveal the essence of the man as most full-length biographies do. States that *The Days Before* will become an enduring piece in American literature.

K. J. "Katherine Anne Porter's Essays Are Joy to Read." *San Antonio Express and News,* 2 Nov. 1952, Sec. C, p. 16, n. col.

Comments that KAP's essays give the reader a special opportunity to know her; states that Texas should be proud that a writer of her ability has her roots in Texas.

Monroe, Harold. "New Porter Collection Is Notable." Rev. of *The Days Before,* by Katherine Anne Porter. *Fort Worth Star-Telegram,* 16 Nov. 1952, Sec. 2, p. 11, col. 2.

States that most Texans are too eager to praise the work of their fellow Texans, but calls praise for KAP most definitely deserved; comments on her ability to write exactly what she wants to say in the most succinct manner so that the reader derives the meaning she wants to convey. Describes her collection of nonfiction pieces as particularly enjoyable because of her views on life and the current scene.

1957

Hendrick, George. "Katherine Anne Porter's 'Noon Wine.'" Rev. of "Noon Wine," by Katherine Anne Porter. *The Texas Observer,* 28 June 1957, p. 6, col. 1–5.

Recalls an incident in KAP's personal life when Dylan Thomas lifted KAP off the ground at a party and refused to release her; Hendrick states that whatever her private life might be, she is a "brilliant craftsman and relentless chronicler of human emotions, motives, and tensions." Traces the origin of the story to KAP's memories from childhood; includes the possible significance in the selection of the characters' names and finds that the story has the only possible ending because all the characters lack the moral strength to redeem themselves. Calls KAP a major American writer.

1958

"Famed Novelist to Inaugurate Program in Criticism Studies." *Daily Texan,* 17 Oct. 1958, Sec. 1, p. 1, col. 5–7.

States that KAP is to open the program of criticism at Texas lecture and seminar series with the topic "'Noon Wine': Its Sources."

"Criticism Scheduled by Writer." *Austin American Statesman,* 19 Oct. 1958, Sec. A, p. 12, col. 4.

Comments that KAP is scheduled to speak on the sources of "Noon Wine" at the University of Texas Program in Criticism; includes biographical data.

"'Noon Wine' To Be Porter's Subject." *Daily Texan,* 19 Oct. 1958, Sec. 1, p. 1, col. 1-2.

Mentions that KAP will speak on "Noon Wine" at University of Texas at Austin.

"Authoress to Discuss 'Noon Wine' Today." *Daily Texan,* 22 Oct. 1958, Sec. 1, p. 1, col. 3-4.

Gives the background of "Noon Wine," set near Austin.

Brewer, Anita. "Novelist Finds Extra Hour." *Austin American Statesman,* 23 Oct. 1958, Sec. 1, p. 1, col. 2-3.

Interviews KAP; describes her personality traits; states that she is an artist who dresses flamboyantly and thinks one should live every moment to the fullest; includes KAP's description of herself as maladjusted regarding organization and "herding," as more feminine than feminist; mentions that she received three doctoral degrees in literature without having attended college.

Jones, Lee. "Novelist Weaves Tale of 'Wine' Inspiration." *Daily Texan,* 23 Oct. 1958, Sec. 1, p. 1, col. 1-3.

Relates incidents from KAP's childhood that provide the background for "Noon Wine," the story of a murderer's need for self-justification.

Bode, Winston. "Miss Porter on Writers and Writing." *The Texas Observer,* 31 Oct. 1958, pp. 6-7.

Interviews KAP in a four-part series; includes her memories of Texas, her views on other writers (James Agee, John Peale Bishop, Allen Tate, and Jesse Stuart), her view of the writer as artist, and the sources of her story "Noon Wine." States that she is the first "serious" writer Texas has produced; states that her birthdate was 1884 instead of 1890; comments that she says that she is not a regional writer because "I don't know any first rate person who is a regional writer." Includes many memories from KAP's childhood.

1959

"Texas-Born Novelist Cancels University Teaching Contract." *Daily Texan,* 4 Aug. 1959, Sec. 1, p. 6, col. 1-2.

Announces that KAP has canceled her contract to teach at the University of Texas in the fall semester of 1959 because of the acceptance of a Ford Foundation grant; states that KAP will continue writing.

Barnes, Lorraine. "Porter Excerpt Gives Quarterly Rich Plum." *Austin American Statesman,* 13 Sept. 1959, Sec. A, p. 17, col. 5–6.

States that KAP is scheduled to publish the first excerpt from her novel *Ship of Fools* in the autumn issue of *Texas Quarterly;* reports that KAP is giving her personal library, manuscripts, and notebooks to the University of Texas.

Barnes, Lorraine. "Books." *Austin American Statesman,* 13 Sept. 1959, Sec. B, p. 1, col. 3.

Mentions that *Ship of Fools* publication has been delayed because of revisions by KAP.

"Quarterly Featuring New Novel." *Austin American Statesman,* 13 Sept. 1959, Sec. A, p. 17, col. 7–9.

Announces that the *Texas Quarterly* will publish a segment of KAP's new novel, *Ship of Fools.*

Tinkle, Lon. "Katherine Anne Porter to Speak at Annual Texas Institute Banquet." *Dallas Morning News,* 5 Nov. 1959, Part IV, p. 7, col. 3–4.

States that KAP is to be the principal speaker at the Texas Institute of Letters Banquet, November 17, 1959.

Tinkle, Lon. "War Shapes Texas Writing: Dobie, Katherine Anne Porter Win Awards." *Dallas Morning News,* 12 Nov. 1959, Part IV, p. 4, col. 3–4.

States that war is the common bond for writers at the Texas Institute of Letters where KAP will be the principal speaker; comments about writers who have recorded stories from World War II, and about KAP being driven from Texas during World War I to become a member of the "Lost Generation."

1961

"Times Praises Terry: More Texas Book News." *Dallas Morning News,* 13 Aug. 1961, Sec. 5, col. 8.

Speculates that KAP's twenty years spent writing *Ship of Fools* may set a record for the length of time to complete a modern novel; states that *Ship of Fools* is scheduled for publication in the spring of 1962.

1962

"Prize Book Taps Texans." *Dallas Morning News,* 4 Mar. 1962, Sec. 5, p. 6, col. 6.

Announces that KAP has won first prize ($300) in the O. Henry Award for her short story "Holiday" published in the *Atlantic Monthly.*

Greene, A. C. "Prediction: Greatness." Rev. of *Ship of Fools,* by Katherine Anne Porter. *Dallas Times Herald,* 1 Apr. 1962, n. sec., n. pag., n. col.

Calls *Ship of Fools* one of the great American literary achievements; describes the book in terms of a fifteenth-century painting by Hieronymus Bosch, a Dutch artist.

Hobby, Diana Poteet. "Varied Entertainment on Life's Journey." Rev. of *Ship of Fools,* by Katherine Anne Porter. *Houston Post,* 1 Apr. 1962, "Houston Now" Sec., p. 22, col. 2–4.

Calls *Ship of Fools* a "rare pleasure for the reader" after the disappointing excerpts that had been published in periodicals; states that the whole of the work transcends the sum of its parts and gives dignity to American fiction.

Tinkle, Lon. "Splendid Fiction from Miss Porter." Rev. of *Ship of Fools,* by Katherine Anne Porter. *Dallas Morning News,* 1 Apr. 1962, Sec. 5, p. 5, col. 1–3.

Describes *Ship of Fools* as a "virtuosic yet disciplined and profoundly serious distillation of a lifetime of concern with people"; calls KAP the greatest living American woman writer; states that none of her characters represent heroic figures but all are studies in mediocrity.

Ledbetter, Nan. "Finally Comes the Novel." *Austin American Statesman,* 8 Apr. 1962, Sec. E, p. 7, col. 8–9.

Gives information on KAP's life, literary career, and reputation as a writer.

Lehan, Richard. "Under the Human Crust." Rev. of *Ship of Fools,* by Katherine Anne Porter. *Austin American Statesman,* 8 Apr. 1962, Sec. E, p. 7, col. 5–7.

Comments that KAP's modern moral allegory forces readers to hate each of the characters in the novel, but only after first hating the same characteristics in themselves; states that she takes the reader on a voyage through life to examine the motives that led the modern world into World War II; calls *Ship of Fools* "devastating" because it is so convincing.

Laswell, Mary. "*Ship of Fools* a Realist's Shocker." Rev. of *Ship of Fools,* by Katherine Anne Porter. *Houston Chronicle,* 15 Apr. 1962, "TV Pullout" Sec., p. 10, col. 2–5.

Calls *Ship of Fools* a microcosm of the horrors of World War II with each of the passengers providing the reader with an accurate picture of the inhumanity of man to man; describes the impressions left on the reader's mind as melancholy and "deep turbulence."

Tinkle, Lon. "SMU Historian John Jones and Katherine Anne Porter." *Dallas Morning News,* 15 Apr. 1962, Sec. 5, p. 6, col. 3–5.

Mentions the influence of Sebastian Brandt's medieval Latin classic on KAP's *Ship of Fools;* includes comments by Professor Jones about KAP and *Ship of Fools.*

James, Jeanette. "Callie Recalled at Indian Creek." *Brownwood Bulletin,* 22 Apr. 1962, n. sec., p. 4, col. 1–5.

Recalls memories of the Porter family while they lived at Indian Creek; mentions the public auction of the Porter household after Alice Porter's death; includes comments on KAP's grandmother Porter; states that KAP claims to be related to Jonathan Boone, brother of Daniel Boone, and to O. Henry (William Sydney Porter).

Tinkle, Lon. "Miss Porter Defines Theme: New Twain; Death in Taos." *Dallas Morning News,* 2 Sept. 1962, Sec. 4, p. 8, col. 4–6.

Seeks to destroy the rumor that KAP spent twenty years of undivided attention on *Ship of Fools;* defines the theme of the novel: Evil exists because good people will not destroy it.

West, Richard. "Behind the Bookshelf." Rev. of *Ship of Fools,* by Katherine Anne Porter. *Daily Texan,* 21 Oct. 1962, Sec. 1, p. 6, col. 5–6.

Comments about KAP's literary reputation and states that she could be considered the "foremost writer in America" if she had published more of her work; describes her style as tough and masculine yet flawless. Includes details from the novel.

Greene, A. C. "'62: Vintage Fiction." *Dallas Times Herald,* 25 Nov. 1962, n. sec., n. pag., n. col.

States that *Ship of Fools* deservedly rates "book of the year" designation; comments on the novel's rich language, passion, style, and reality.

1963

"Women Sweep Awards at Texas Institute Meet." *Dallas Morning News,* 17 Feb. 1963, Sec. 6, p. 11, col. 4–5.

Announces that KAP received for *Ship of Fools* the $1,000 Jesse H. Jones Award at the Texas Institute of Letters in San Antonio.

"News Critics Pick Winners." *Dallas Morning News,* 17 Feb. 1963, Sec. 6, p. 11, col. 4.

Includes Lon Tinkle's commentary on *Ship of Fools* as the winner of the Jesse H. Jones Award.

Laswell, Mary. "Katherine Anne Porter Takes Jones Award." *Houston Chronicle,* 17 Feb. 1963, Sec. 1, p. 13, col. 1–8.

Announces that KAP has been awarded the first Jesse H. Jones Award for *Ship of Fools;* includes report of the award presentation and KAP's speech.

Tinkle, Lon. "Miss Porter Chose Mexico, Not Paris." *Dallas Morning News,* 28 Apr. 1963, Sec. 1, p. 25, col. 3–4.

Comments on KAP's avoiding the "Lost Generation" of writers by moving to Mexico and asserting her individuality.

"'Ship' Again Overlooked." *Dallas Times Herald,* 12 May 1963, n. sec. n. pag. n. col.

Mentions failure of *Ship of Fools* to win either the Pulitzer Prize or the National Book Award for fiction this year.

Tinkle, Lon. "Great Exhibition Plus Miss Porter." *Dallas Morning News,* 29 Dec. 1963, Sec. 4, p. 6, col. 7–8.

Reports that KAP is to speak at the Texas Institute of Letters on February 15, 1964; includes KAP's literary history.

1964

"Personal Mention." *Houston Chronicle,* 5 Feb. 1964, Sec. 2, p. 1, col. 1.

Comments that KAP is to address the Texas Institute of Letters in Dallas on February 15.

"Katherine Anne Porter to Lecture Here Thursday." *Dallas Times Herald,* 8 Feb. 1964, n. sec., n. pag., n. col.

Announces that KAP is to speak at SMU and the Texas Institute of Letters on February 15.

Bode, Winston. "Tall in Texas." *Houston Chronicle,* 9 Feb. 1964, "Zest" Sec., p. 16, col. 1.

Mentions that KAP is to visit Dallas on February 15 to give an address to the Texas Institute of Letters banquet.

Tinkle, Lon. "Miss Porter Here: At SMU and TIL." *Dallas Morning News,* 9 Feb. 1964, Sec. 4, p. 5, col. 3–4.

States that KAP will speak at SMU and the Texas Institute of Letters on February 15; includes biographical and literary history of KAP.

"'Ship' Idled 10 Years." *Dallas Times Herald,* 13 Feb. 1964, n. sec., n. pag., n. col.

Interviews KAP who arrived in Dallas for her speaking engagement at SMU and Texas Institute of Letters; retraces the development of *Ship of Fools* through twenty years of note taking and planning; includes literary history.

"Novelist Porter Talks of Craft." *Dallas Morning News,* 14 Feb. 1964, Sec. 1, p. 14, col. 1–3.

Interviews KAP in Dallas; includes her opinions of writers who write pornography "for dirt's sake" and "wallow publicly in their own unhappy pasts."

"People." *Austin American Statesman,* 17 Feb. 1964, Sec. 1, p. 9, col. 3.

Mentions that KAP is recuperating in Dallas from a respiratory ailment that forced her to cancel a speaking engagement.

"Personal Mention." *Houston Chronicle,* 17 Feb. 1964, Sec. 2, p. 1, col. 1.

States that KAP was forced to cancel her speaking engagement for the Texas Institute of Letters because of a respiratory illness.

Tinkle, Lon. "Spunk of KAP and Her Credo." *Dallas Morning News,* 23 Feb. 1964, Sec. 7, p. 2, col. 1–2.

Gives an account of KAP's illness that forced her to cancel speaking engagements at SMU and the Texas Institute of Letters; includes an interview with KAP from her hospital room at St. Paul's Hospital in Dallas; mentions her artistic credo.

Holmes, Charles. "Stories on a Story Teller." *Dallas Times Herald,* 8 Mar. 1964, n. sec., n. pag., n. col.

> Describes reputation KAP made while staying at St. Paul's Hospital in Dallas; calls KAP "regal," "queenly," and says that she disliked being called a regional writer.

Tinkle, Lon. "Ambivalent Art of Miss Porter." Rev. of *Katherine Anne Porter and the Art of Rejection,* by William L. Nance. *Dallas Morning News,* 8 Mar. 1964, Sec. 3, p. 8, col. 1–3.

> States that Nance's *Katherine Anne Porter and the Art of Rejection* is one of the "most acute and sensitive works of literary criticism by a Texan," but that in his criticism of KAP's flights from oppressive circumstances, it is Nance who is rejecting art rather than KAP rejecting truth.

Tinkle, Lon. "NBA's New Prize: Porter, Dobie." *Dallas Morning News,* 15 Mar. 1964, Sec. 7, p. 2, col. 6–7.

> Announces that KAP won the National Book Award prize; speculates over whether she will return to Texas to live as she has indicated that she would like to; states that she will be the subject of a special issue of *The Texas Observer.*

Tinkle, Lon. "A Writer Loyal to Real Experience." *The Texas Observer,* 24 Jul. 1964, p. 9.

> Mentions KAP in a tribute to J. Frank Dobie: "Miss Porter said, in essence, that she was the first and only Texas-born writer to achieve international fame as an artist in the European sense of the word. Miss Porter, an eminently sensible woman, was careful to point out that she was not referring to herself as a 'genius', as the careless would assume. She is a novelist and short-story writer of flawless craft, admired and appreciated all over the world."

1965

Tinkle, Lon. "Texans Continue Making Book News." *Dallas Morning News,* 25 Apr. 1965, Sec. 4, p. 11, col. 2.

> Announces that KAP will be the subject of a special issue of *The Texas Observer.*

Wichita Falls Times, 19 Sept. 1965, "Feature Magazine," p. 4, n. col.

> States that KAP's ability to blend characterization and specific detail makes each incident in her work a memorable reading experience.

1966

Ashford, Gerald. "Books and Art." *San Antonio Express and News,* 9 Jan. 1966, Sec. H, p. 6, n. col.

Comments on a letter from KAP about her birthplace, Indian Creek, Texas.

"Katherine Anne Porter Tells Editor about Her Birthplace." *San Antonio Express and News,* 13 Mar. 1966, Sec. H, p. 4, n. col.

Comments on a letter from KAP about her birthplace; states that her home did not make a mark on her memory.

Miller, Joy. "Katherine Anne Porter Receives National Book Award for Fiction." *Dallas Morning News,* 16 Mar. 1966, Sec. C, p. 2, col. 1–3.

Announces that KAP at age seventy-five won the seventeenth annual National Book Award for fiction for her *Collected Stories;* includes biographical data.

Smith, Miles A. "'Texan Also a Winner', Arthur Schlesinger Honored for Book on President Kennedy." *Houston Chronicle,* 16 Mar. 1966, Sec. 2, p. 3, col. 1–3.

Announces that KAP won the fiction prize (for *The Collected Stories of Katherine Anne Porter*) from the National Book Awards, a project of three trade groups in the book-publishing industry.

Miller, Joy. "Book Prize Winner Is Phenom, 75." *Austin American Statesman,* 17 Mar. 1966, Sec. A, p. 46, col. 1.

Interviews KAP after winning the National Book Award. Relates KAP's views on popularity as a writer, money, growing old, and the serious nature of writing.

Tinkle, Lon. "Drama Plus Style: Miss Porter, NBA." *Dallas Morning News,* 20 Mar. 1966, Sec. E, p. 8, col. 3–5.

Comments on KAP winning the National Book Award for fiction; states that she is the first Texan to win the award; includes controversy over the eligibility of her *Collected Stories* to receive the award.

"Miss Porter Gets Last Word." *San Antonio Express and News,* 3 Apr. 1966, Sec. H, p. 8, n. col.

Includes a commentary on a letter from KAP to the book review editor, Gerald Ashford, clarifying any misconception about her personal history.

Naylor, Pauline. "Katherine Anne Porter's Days Recalled." *Fort Worth Star-Telegram,* 10 Apr. 1966, Sec. 5, n. pag., col. 3–8.

Gives the recollections of Miss Beniti McElwee, a friend of KAP's during World War I. Includes segments of KAP's reportage of society events for *The Critic* in Fort Worth; includes picture of KAP performing at the Little Theater in Fort Worth.

"14 Pulitzer Awards for 1966 Announced." *Houston Chronicle,* 3 May 1966, Sec. 1, p. 11, col. 2–4.

Announces that KAP received the Pulitzer Prize for fiction for *The Collected Stories of Katherine Anne Porter.*

"Plus the Pulitzer." *Dallas Morning News,* 8 May 1966, Sec. F, p. 10, col. 5–6.

Announces that KAP won the Pulitzer Prize for fiction for her volume, *Collected Stories;* mentions that the award came shortly after she had won the National Book Award for fiction.

Mort, John. "Novelist Porter Irked at UT." *Fort Worth Star-Telegram,* 18 Dec. 1966, Sec. A, p. 13, col. 4–8.

States that KAP will donate her manuscripts and papers to the University of Maryland because of a misunderstanding with Chancellor Harry Ransom of the University of Texas; includes KAP's claims that Ransom had promised to set aside a room named for her collection, but the room was never named for KAP.

"Writer Says UT's Ransom Snubbed Her." *Houston Chronicle,* 18 Dec. 1966, Sec. 2, p. 13, col. 1.

Reports KAP's claim that Harry Ransom, chancellor of the University of Texas, would not reply to her letters; therefore, KAP is giving the collection of her papers to the University of Maryland; includes statement that Ransom denies ever having had any communication with KAP.

1967

Tinkle, Lon. "New Texas Loss: KAP Collection." *Dallas Morning News,* 1 Jan. 1967, Sec. C, p. 8, col. 1–2.

Announces that KAP stated during the Christmas holidays that she will give her papers and manuscripts to the University of Maryland. Calls loss of KAP collection "as stunning a blow as the deplorable loss to Yale some years back of the great Streeter collection of Texana." Comments that KAP decided on Maryland when President Wilson H. Elkins (a former University of Texas football player) personally traveled to her home to award KAP an honorary degree from Maryland.

1970

"Pale Horse, Clear Voice." *Dallas Times Herald,* 12 Apr. 1970, n. sec., n. pag., n. col.

Gives KAP's views on sex, women's liberation, youth, and old age.

Benchley, Peter. "Katherine Anne Porter Grande Dame of American Letters." *Austin American Statesman,* 19 Apr. 1970, Sec. F, p. 13, col. 1-4.

Details KAP's literary career.

Tinkle, Lon. "KAP Collection: Dazzling Essays." Rev. of *The Collected Essays and Occasional Writings of Katherine Anne Porter,* by Katherine Anne Porter. *Dallas Morning News,* 26 Apr. 1970, Sec. 7, p. 10, col. 1-2.

Calls KAP's essays a "magnificent success"; describes the essays concerning Cotton Mather as following the basic theme of her short stories — man's inhumanity to man; comments on the other essays individually and states that the variety of ideas presented provide the reader with ample food for thought.

1971

Houston Chronicle, 6 Apr. 1971, n. sec., n. pag., n. col.

Comments on KAP's speech at a women's conference in Baltimore; states that she feels the majority of women do not value themselves as women; mentions that she does not follow the women's liberation movement because the followers seem to "be men haters."

1972

Buckley, Tom. "'Ship of Fools' Author Reigns on Cruise with Mailer." *Fort Worth Star-Telegram,* 17 Dec. 1972, Sec. 1, p. 5, col. 1-6.

Reports that KAP and Norman Mailer were aboard the SS *Statendam* covering the launch of Apollo 17; states that the eighty-two-year-old KAP was on assignment for *Playboy Magazine.*

1973

"Apollo." *Houston Post,* 14 Jan. 1973, "Spotlight" Sec., pp. 7-8, col. 3-5.

Comments by KAP and Norman Mailer on the launching of Apollo 17; states that she and Mailer were on board the SS *Statendam* off the coast of Cape Kennedy; includes the opinions of both Mailer and KAP on the feasibility of the space program; states that she felt the launch was an overwhelming event, almost a mystical experience.

"Mary Porter Hillendahl Services on Tuesday." *Houston Chronicle*, 21 May 1973, Sec. 4, p. 5, col. 5–6.

Gives the details of the funeral services for Mary Porter Hillendahl, sister of KAP.

1974

Allen, Henry. "Coffin's Ready." *Austin American Statesman,* 30 June 1974, "The Show World" Sec., p. 43, col. 1–2.

Mentions that KAP has ordered her coffin from a mail-order carpenter shop in Arizona; includes biographical information.

Allen, Henry. "A Visit with Katherine Anne Porter." *Dallas Times Herald,* 3 Jul. 1974, Sec. 6, p. 1, col. 5–6.

Interviews KAP as she recalls events in her life; mentions the coffin she has ordered from the mail-order carpenter in Arizona.

Allen, Henry. "Katherine Anne Porter Has Bought Her Coffin and Keeps It in Her Hall Closet." *Houston Chronicle,* 7 Jul. 1974, "Books Section," pp. 1 and 12, col. 1–4.

Interviews KAP; describes the coffin she bought from a mail-order carpenter in Arizona; includes comments about her Texas family and heritage.

1976

"Porter Seminar Set March 8–26." *The Yellow Jacket,* 27 Feb. 1976, Sec. 1, pp. 1 and 4, col. 1.

States that a special seminar to study KAP's work will be held March 8–26 at Howard Payne University in Brownwood, Texas, in preparation for the symposium honoring KAP that is to be held May 10–11. (*The Yellow Jacket* is the student newspaper at Howard Payne University.)

Givner, Joan. "A Fine Day of Homage to Porter." *Dallas Morning News,* 23 May 1976, Sec. G, p. 5, col. 1–4.

Describes the events at the Katherine Anne Porter Symposium held in Brownwood, Texas, at Howard Payne University.

1977

Barkham, John. "Book Marks Anniversary of Executions." Rev. of *The Never-Ending Wrong,* by Katherine Anne Porter. *Wichita Falls Record News,* 18 Aug. 1977, n. sec., n. pag., n. col.

Calls *The Never-Ending Wrong* a dated publication showing through its lines the memories of the 1920s; states that in KAP's view the execution of Sacco and Vanzetti was symptomatic of the change in the American people, but that KAP is naive in her viewpoint in light of the worldwide massacres from war and persecution.

Morris, Donald R. "'Persistent Controversy', Review of *The Never-Ending Wrong* by Katherine Anne Porter." *Houston Post,* 28 Aug. 1977, "Spotlight" Sec., p. 32, col. 1–7.

Calls KAP's book a "short account . . . about participation in the protest" (Sacco-Vanzetti); states that the book delves more deeply into KAP's remembrance of the fellow protesters at the Sacco-Vanzetti trial than about the accused men themselves.

"'Voyage' of Novelist Traced." *The Victoria Advocate,* 7 Sept. 1977, Sec. A, p. 1, col. 4–8; p. 16, col. 4–8.

Describes the research of Dr. Joan Givner of the University of Regina, Saskatchewan, into the life history of KAP; mentions that Givner visited Victoria, Texas.

1979

Givner, Joan. "Katherine Anne Porter's Texas." *Vision,* 2, no. 10 (Sept., 1979), pp. 18–22.

Relates KAP's Texas background from her birth to the time of her death; includes her return trips to Texas to visit and her attitudes toward Texas, and mentions her long-time rivalry with J. Frank Dobie; emphasizes the importance of Texas in KAP's life.

1980

"Prize-Winning Author Dead at 90." *Austin American Statesman,* 19 Sept. 1980, Sec. A, p. 5, col. 1–2.

Announces KAP's death in College Park, Maryland.

"Pulitzer-Winning Author Katherine Anne Porter Dies." *Houston Chronicle,* 19 Sept. 1980, Sec. 2, p. 9, col. 6–7.

Announces KAP's death Thursday, September 18, 1980; calls her one of the greatest American writers of short stories; states she lived for a time in Houston and wrote *Pale Horse, Pale Rider* while living in Houston.

"Author Dies at 90." *San Angelo Standard Times,* 19 Sept. 1980, n. sec., n. pag., n. col.

Announces KAP's death.

"Novelist Dies at 90." *The Victoria Advocate,* 19 Sept. 1980, Sec. A, p. 8, col. 6.

Comments on the death of KAP at age ninety.

Laughlin, Charlotte. "HPU Professor Looks into Life of Author." *Brownwood Bulletin,* 21 Sept. 1980, Sec. A, p. 1, col. 5–8.

Gives the details of KAP's family background in Indian Creek, Texas; includes previously unknown facts about KAP's relatives and family history.

"Ashes of Porter Will be Buried in Central Texas." *Houston Chronicle,* 21 Sept. 1980, Sec. 4, p. 6, col. 4.

States that KAP's body is to be cremated and then buried in a private ceremony next to her mother's grave in Indian Creek, Texas.

Laughlin, Charlotte. "Porter Anticipated Death." *Brownwood Bulletin,* 22 Sept. 1980, Sec. A, p. 1, col. 3–6; p. 2, col. 6.

Comments that KAP's life was built on myth and that the myth continued with her death; states that her wish to be buried next to her mother whom she did not know rather than her father whom she did know is indicative of the strength of myth in her life. Calls KAP's return to Texas for burial the full circle of her life, a return to the home she never found elsewhere in all of her other moves throughout the years.

1981

Milazzo, Lee. "The Colorful Life and Career of Katherine Anne Porter." Rev. of *Conversations with Katherine Anne Porter,* by Enrique Hank Lopez. *Dallas Morning News,* 12 Jul. 1981, Sec. G, p. 4, col. 1–5.

States that in the absence of a biography of KAP Lopez's book "whets the appetite" for a full-scale biography of the complicated KAP. Mentions that the book leaves the reader wondering about the details of situations that are merely alluded to by Lopez.

Brunsdale, Mitzi. "Needed But Not Satisfying Study of KAP." Rev. of *Conversations with Katherine Anne Porter,* by Enrique Hank Lopez. *Houston Post,* 23 Aug. 1981, Sec. AA, p. 18, col. 1–4.

States that Lopez's book fills a need to supply KAP's readers with minor information about her; mentions the problem Lopez recognizes in KAP's need to confuse fantasy with reality in the details of her life.

McMurtry, Larry. "Ever a Bridegroom: Reflections on the Failure of Texas Literature." *The Texas Observer,* 23 Oct. 1981, pp. 1, 8–12.

States that KAP is the Texas writer usually cited as a major writer, but then proceeds to demonstrate why she is not major; calls her style "purified almost to the vanishing point" and states that she provided "inscrutable" rather than "impeccable" fiction; provides an analysis of other Texas writers.

Biffle, Kent. "Bulldozing Texas' Literary Landscape." *Dallas Morning News,* 8 Nov. 1981, Sec. G, p. 1, col. 1–5.

Comments on Larry McMurtry's article in *The Texas Observer* which stated that "Texas has produced no major writers or major books." Mentions that McMurtry reminds readers that KAP's fiction is "beautiful plumage" but that plumage is actually "only feathers."

1982

Givner, Joan. "The Lady From Indian Creek." *The Texas Observer,* 7 May 1982, pp. 29–30.

Responds to the article in *The Texas Observer* by Larry McMurtry; defends KAP's position as a major writer in American literature; states that KAP truthfully confronted the pain in her own life and converted it into a realistic fiction; calls her a writer's writer whose place in American letters was secured long before KAP's death in 1980.

Rigler, Judyth. "The Best on Texas." *Bryan–College Station Eagle,* 2 Oct. 1982, "Saturday Magazine" Sec., p. 16, col. 1–2.

Reviews A. C. Greene's *The 50 Best Books on Texas;* includes anecdote about KAP refusing to admit that she worked for the *Dallas News:* "I have always thought it strange she was so bitter in her disavowal of things Texan, yet did so many of her best stories with a Texas background."

Hunter, William B., Jr. "Katherine Anne Porter: The Real Person, the Real Feelings." Rev. of *Katherine Anne Porter: A Life,* by

Joan Givner. *Houston Chronicle,* 12 Dec. 1982, "Zest" Sec., p. 19, n. col.

Calls KAP Texas' greatest writer; mentions her childhood in Indian Creek and Kyle, Texas, and her marriage to the son of a rancher from Victoria, Texas (John Henry Koontz). States that Givner has performed a great service in separating the fact of KAP's life from the fictional accounts KAP often gave.

1983

Popkin-Paine, Linda. "Callie Becomes Katherine, Her Life Becomes Her Art." Rev. of *Katherine Anne Porter: A Life,* by Joan Givner. *Houston Post,* 2 Jan. 1983, Sec. G, p. 16, col. 1–4.

Calls Givner's biography a well-documented account of the "most remarkable writer to come out of Texas." States that Givner binds the facts of KAP's life with the fiction she created; gives basic details of KAP's life from the book.

1984

Biondo, Anne Marie. "Gift Epitomizes Childhood." *Fort Worth Star-Telegram,* 16 Apr. 1984, Sec. B, p. 1, col. 1–4; p. 4, col. 2–3.

Offers insight into KAP's early life through a photograph taken of the Porter children when KAP was two. Mentions that a neighbor in Indian Creek did not find the picture valuable and that the mother's face was veiled. Quotes George Hendrick that the circumstances typify the rejection that KAP often felt. Announces the University of Texas at Arlington conference on Southern and Southwestern writers.

Watson, Keith. "Location Filming for 'Noon Wine' Version Authentic." *Houston Post,* 26 Jul. 1984, Sec. F, p. 1, col. 1.

States that filming began Wednesday, July 25, at a farm near Stonewall, Texas, for public television's *American Playhouse* version of "Noon Wine." Lists the principal actors as Fred Ward, Lise Hilboldt, Pat Hingle, and Stellan Skarsgard, with Michael Field directing. Comments that this is the second film adaptation of "Noon Wine." The earlier version, which starred Jason Robards and Per Oscarsson, had revived Sam Peckinpah's career as a director.

1985

Compton, Robert. "Addenda." *Dallas Morning News,* 8 Apr. 1985, Sec. G, p. 5.

Announces the Katherine Anne Porter Memorial Lectures at the University of Texas at Arlington, April II. Includes the speakers and topics: Cleanth Brooks, "Romantic Personality, Disciplined Art"; George Hendrick, "Katherine Anne Porter's Texas"; Dorothy Walters, "Female Initiation and Self-Discovery in Porter's Fiction"; and a discussion, "Katherine Anne Porter—A Revaluation," featuring Hendrick, Brooks, Walters, and James Lee.

1987

Milazzo, Lee. "Writers Talk: Embellishing on the Art of Storytelling." *Dallas Morning News,* 13 Dec. 1987, n. sec., n. pag., n. col.

Review of Givner's *Katherine Anne Porter: Conversations.* Recommends Givner's book as an excellent source for understanding the myths Porter created about her life as well as the art she created.

n. d. (possibly 1956)

Blackburn, Louis. "Medium Rare." *Houston Press,* n. d., n. sec., n. pag., n. col.

Comments on KAP; describes her work and her taste in food; states that she makes Hoppinjohn for New Year's Day and likes hominy grits, cornbread, fried chicken, hot biscuits, sweet potatoes, cucumbers, tomatoes, corn on the cob, peaches, and watermelon.

2. *Journal Articles Published in Texas*

1940

Crume, Paul. Rev. of *Pale Horse, Pale Rider,* by Katherine Anne Porter. *Southwest Review,* 25 (1940), pp. 213–18.

Calls KAP's writing a "connoisseur's product" that is a unique blending of impressionism and journalistic reporting. Includes extensive biographical information about KAP with remembrances of people who knew her in Dallas; concludes that "Old Mortality" is the strongest story of the three stories in *Pale Horse, Pale Rider.*

1956

Allen, Charles A. "Katherine Anne Porter: Psychology as Art." *Southwest Review,* 41, no. 3 (1956), pp. 223–30.

Gives the psychological ramifications attached to characters from "The Downward Path to Wisdom," "The Cracked Looking-Glass," "Maria Concepción," "The Jilting of Granny Weatherall," "Hacienda," and "Flowering Judas."

1960

Schwartz, Edward Greenfield. "The Fiction of Memory." *Southwest Review*, 45, no. 4 (1960), pp. 204–215.

Traces how KAP attempts to create reality in her work through consciousness of the individual, particularly in the Miranda stories; asserts that KAP wants to recover order through consciousness.

1968

Fortenberry, George E. Rev. of *Katherine Anne Porter*, by George Hendrick. *Arlington Quarterly*, 1 (1968), pp. 250–52.

States that Hendrick is able to show KAP as an artist whose dedication to truth as she saw it is apparent in the treatment of her subjects; book serves as an effective guide to understanding KAP's sources, motives, and commitment to art; includes previously unknown biographical information. (*Arlington Quarterly* is published by the University of Texas at Arlington.)

1969

Gross, Barry. Rev. of *The Art of Southern Fiction*, by Frederick J. Hoffman. *Studies in the Novel*, 1 (1969), p. 377.

Includes KAP in a group of Southern writers who are treated as unique individuals with special emphasis on each writer's peculiar strengths.

1970

McDowell, Judith H. Rev. of *Katherine Anne Porter: A Critical Symposium*, ed. Lodwick Harley and George Core. *Arlington Quarterly*, 2 (1970), pp. 200–201.

Praises Hartley and Core for their ability to select readable and perceptive articles about KAP that delineate KAP's contribution to American literature.

Nance, William L. "Katherine Anne Porter and Mexico." *Southwest Review*, 55, no. 2 (1970), pp. 143–53.

Analyzes the role of Mexico in KAP's literary career; includes "Maria Concepción," "Virgin Violeta," "The Martyr," *Ship of Fools*, plus four other short stories and several essays dealing with Mexico. Links the revolutionary spirit of Mexico and KAP's desire for freedom.

1972

Hernandez, Frances. "Katherine Anne Porter and Julio Cortazár: The Craft of Fiction." In *Modern American Fiction, Insights and*

Foreign Lights. Vol. 5 of *Proceedings of the Comparative Literature Symposium.* Ed. Wolodymyr T. Zyla and Wendell M. Aycock. Lubbock: Texas Tech Press, 1972, pp. 55–66.

Focuses on the similarities of the two writers: translators, rebels in both their personal lives and work. Both are obsessed with perfection in work and interested in symbolism and death. They share the same genre, and both have the desire to remain free from literary influence.

1973

Gaston, Edwin W. "The Mythic South of Katherine Anne Porter." *Southwestern American Literature,* 3 (1973), pp. 81–85.

Analyzes the Southern myth theme that KAP, much like Faulkner, confronts in her stories "The Old Order" and "Old Mortality." States that KAP reveals the flaws in the Southern myth with her confrontation of both the positive and the negative myths. (*Southwestern American Literature* is published by North Texas State University, Denton, Texas.)

1974

Givner, Joan. "Porter's Subsidiary Art." *Southwest Review,* 59, no. 3 (1974), pp. 265–76.

Reviews KAP's letters, which have been donated to the University of Maryland's McKeldin Library; includes the development of *Ship of Fools.*

Gray, R. J. "The Grace of Pure Awareness: Katherine Anne Porter." *Southwestern American Literature,* 4 (1974), pp. 1–13.

Traces the theme of development of consciousness in KAP's fiction; states that her method always involves the examination of a myth in terms of the restrictions it imposes, counterbalanced with the needs of the individual, and the result is a new awareness within the protagonist.

1975

Shurbutt, S. "The Short Fiction of Katherine Anne Porter: Mementos de Verdades." *Southwestern American Literature,* 5 (1975), pp. 40–46.

Analyzes "Virgin Violeta," "Maria Concepción," "Hacienda," "The Cracked Looking-Glass," and "Old Mortality" to show how KAP uses the "moment of truth" to awaken an individual to the reality that is around him and how that moment of realization permanently alters the person's life.

1976

Donalson, Dawn. "Texas Trailblazer." *The Sting* (Spring 1976), pp. 8–9.

Comments on KAP's work and philosophy of life. (*The Sting* is the fine arts magazine of Howard Payne University, Brownwood, Texas.)

Smith, Charles W. "A Flaw in Katherine Anne Porter's 'Theft': The Teacher Taught." *CEA Critic: An Official Journal of the College English Association,* 38, no. 2 (1976), pp. 19–21.

States that KAP's use of an improper tense in the opening sentence of "Theft" causes confusion in the mind of the reader and results in a lack of understanding of the flashback technique KAP uses in the story. States that this story is worth teaching because it demonstrates that professional writers make mistakes and that those mistakes result in serious misunderstandings.

1977

Givner, Joan. "'Her Art, Her Sober Craft': Katherine Anne Porter's Creative Process." *Southwest Review,* 62, no. 3 (1977), pp. 217–30.

Explains KAP's creative process of writing by the utilization of factual origins in the stories; includes anecdotes from KAP's life.

Groff, Edward. "'Noon Wine': A Texas Tragedy." *Descant,* 22 (Fall 1977), pp. 39–47.

States that KAP's fiction is an American adaptation of the ancient view of tragedy whereby the hero is not bound by sociological or psychological forces but struggles to arrive at an understanding of moral issues through his own initiative. Applies the principles of Aristotelian tragedy to the characters in "Noon Wine." States that the dimensions of moral significance extend beyond the plot of the story.

Stern, Carol Simpson. "'A Flaw in Katherine Anne Porter's "Theft": The Teacher Taught'—A Reply." *CEA Critic: An Official Journal of the College English Association,* 39, no. 4 (1977), pp. 4–8.

Asserts that KAP deliberately chose the past tense in the opening sentence of "Theft" rather than the past perfect, as Charles W. Smith suggested in his article, in order that the story might slowly unfold for the reader; includes an analysis of the complex relationship between protagonist and implied author in the story.

Smith, Charles W. "Rebuttal." *CEA Critic: An Official Journal of the College English Association,* 39, no. 4 (1977), pp. 9–11.

Refuses to accept Stern's theory that the ambiguity in the first paragraph of "Theft" is intentional and necessary to the story's complexity; analyzes the protagonist in the story to dispute the theory that a misleading statement in the first sentence is called for to accentuate the complexity of the protagonist-implied author relationship.

1978

Givner, Joan. "'The Plantation of This Isle': Katherine Anne Porter's Bermuda Base." *Southwest Review,* 63, no. 4 (1978), pp. 339–51.

Describes KAP's Bermuda home, but also emphasizes her Texas roots. Mentions the discrepancy between KAP's accounts of her home and property and the recollections of the people who knew the Porter family in the early 1900s.

1979

Givner, Joan. "Katherine Anne Porter, Journalist." *Southwest Review,* 64, no. 4 (1979), pp. 309–321.

States that the reporting technique in KAP's fiction was enhanced by her working as a reporter for the *Fort Worth Critic,* and that her personal experiences colored her writing.

1983

Givner, Joan. "Katherine Anne Porter: The Old Order and the New." In Don Graham, James W. Lee, and William T. Pilkington, eds., *The Texas Literary Tradition: Fiction, Folklore, and History.* Proceedings from the Conference on Texas Literature, University of Texas at Austin, 24–26 Mar. 1983.

Considers the reasons KAP was passed over for the Best Book Award by the Texas Institute of Letters in 1939. Attributes Dobie's win to the masculine establishment in Texas literature. Takes issue with McMurtry's article "Ever A Bridegroom." Points to the sometimes disclaimed debt and relationship between KAP and William Humphrey and William Goyen. Concludes that KAP was significant because she extended the realm of Texas literature beyond a totally masculine domain.

1984

Givner, Joan. "Katherine Anne Porter: Queen of Texas Letters?" *Texas Libraries,* 45 (Winter 1984), pp. 119–23.

Addresses the issue of Porter's betrayal of Josephine Herbst to the FBI. Surmises what could have happened to cause Porter to reveal confidences to the FBI; examines KAP's behavior in relation to one of her themes in writing—abhorrence of betrayal; argues for KAP's place in Texas writing.

1985

Leath, Helen L. "Washing the Dirty Linen in Private: An Analysis of Katherine Anne Porter's 'Magic.'" *Conference of College Teachers of English of Texas,* 5 (1985), pp. 51-57.

Refutes the interpretation of Nance, Hendrick, and Givner. Argues that "Magic" may best be interpreted as the battle for supremacy between two women: Madame Blanchard and the narrator-maid. Finds that the maid uses the example of Ninette to subjugate Madame Blanchard and thus keep her job secure. Mentions "Maria Concepción" and "The Jilting of Granny Weatherall" as other Porter works that have the struggle for dominance as their theme.

C. Theses, Dissertations, and Symposium Presentations

1. *Theses*

1951

Irby, Hazel M. "Katherine Anne Porter: Her Contribution to the American Short Story." M.A. thesis, University of Texas, 1951.

Examines the short stories of KAP to emphasize the value of KAP's contribution to the modern short story. Includes biography, sources and influences for KAP, and analyses of plot, structure, characterization, settings, style, and values.

Stalling, Donald. "Katherine Anne Porter: Life and Literary Mirror." M.A. thesis, Texas Christian University, 1951.

Examines incidents in KAP's life that are reflected in the stories she wrote to demonstrate what can be done with the fragments of life in the hands of a "creator in the world of literature."

1957

Council, Mary J. "The Collected Fiction of Katherine Anne Porter: A Doubter's World in Miniature." M.A. thesis, University of Texas at El Paso, 1957.

Examines KAP's fiction in terms of literary influences, unifying themes and backgrounds, "slice of life" technique, and her underlying philosophy.

1958

Robbins, Orville M. "'True Testimony': The Short Stories of Katherine Anne Porter." M.A. thesis, Texas Christian University, 1958.

Examines KAP's work from the standpoint of its basic meanings; includes her critical reputation; analyzes the stories in terms of surface aspects and enveloping action; focuses on character, narration, complication, and resolution. Concludes with an examination of major themes in the totality of her fiction.

1959

Speer, Mary T. "Four Women Writers of the Southwest (Katherine Anne Porter, Mary Austin, Dorothy Scarborough, and L. Grace Erdman)." M.A. thesis, University of Texas at El Paso, 1959.

Examines the influence the Southwest may have had on the writings of KAP, Austin, Scarborough, and Erdman. Deals specifically with the question of whether or not the Southwest made them different from Pearl Buck or Ellen Glasgow. Emphasizes style, characterization, subject matter, and interpretation of the Southwest scene.

1961

Wilson, Florence Janet. "The Narrative Technique of Katherine Anne Porter." M.A. thesis, Baylor University, 1961.

Examines KAP's "Mexican stories" and "The Old Order" to determine how the narrative technique and style are the vehicles for KAP's message.

1963

Grau, Carolyn. "Major Themes in the Fiction of Katherine Anne Porter." M.A. thesis, Texas Tech University, 1963.

Divides KAP's themes into concern with the past, delusions and disillusionments, alienation, despair and confusion, and violence. Examines her fiction through themes.

1965

Ewing, Mary D. "Regionalism in the Short Works of Katherine Anne Porter." M.A. thesis, Texas Christian University, 1965.

Includes a brief personal and literary biography of KAP; defines regionalism, and examines KAP's short stories in relation to the South and Southwest in terms of dialect, use of history, customs, moral codes, characterization, and setting.

Sewell, Joan D. "The Theme of Isolation in Stories by Katherine Anne Porter." M.A. thesis, University of Houston, 1965.

Analyzes the theme of psychological isolation as it applies to the child, the adolescent, and the young adult. Examines "He," "The Downward Path to Wisdom," "The Circus," "The Fig Tree," "The Grave," "Old Mortality," and "Pale Horse, Pale Rider" to demonstrate KAP's persistent theme of isolation and its counterpart, the quest for personal identity.

1966

Lackey, Horace G. "Katherine Anne Porter's Theory of Art as Revealed in Her Life and Work." M.A. thesis, Texas Tech University, 1966.

Examines art as it applies to KAP's life and literary career, notably through the artists and objets d'art in her fiction.

Maass, Henry E. "Mexico and Mexicans in the Fiction of Steinbeck, Morris, Traven, and Porter." M.A. thesis, North Texas State University, 1966.

Investigates principal attitudes of Americans toward Mexico and Mexicans as demonstrated through the writings of Steinbeck, Morris, Traven, and KAP.

1968

Ferguson, S. M. "Katherine Anne Porter's Fiction: Man in a Falling World." M.A. thesis, North Texas State University, 1968.

Attempts to demonstrate that KAP's *Ship of Fools* is not a departure from her previous work, but the culmination in theme and technical skill of all of her short fiction. Examines the short stories that foreshadow the novel and then analyzes the novel to determine the exact vision KAP presents.

1969

Brewton, Constance D. "Miranda's Quest: Katherine Anne Porter's Portrayal of Woman." M.A. thesis, University of Dallas, 1969.

Parallels mankind's quest for identity with Miranda's quest in the Miranda stories of KAP.

1972

Isbell, Carol. "A Study of Women in Katherine Anne Porter's 'Miranda' Stories." M.A. thesis, Texas Woman's University, 1972.

Gives extensive biographical data on KAP; analyzes the female characters in the Miranda stories to demonstrate how they contribute to a more complete understanding of Miranda; explores Miranda's personality as she becomes a "literary window" through whom life in the South is seen; demonstrates the struggle to find identity in childhood, adolescence, and young adulthood through an analysis of the 'Miranda' stories.

James, Almola. "Maria Concepción, Laura, and Julia: The Role of Necessity in Rejection." M.A. thesis, Howard Payne University, 1972.

Studies the question, "How can one live in a world where neither society nor the universe offers any meaning or love?" through the actions and attitudes of Maria, Dona Julia, and Laura in KAP's fiction. (Material from this thesis was given as a lecture at the Katherine Anne Porter Symposium, May 10-11, 1976, at Howard Payne University.)

1973

Fitzgerald, Joanne. "The Comic Irony of Katherine Anne Porter." M.A. thesis, University of Dallas, 1973.

Asserts that in portraying modern life, KAP's view is essentially comic and parallels the comic theme of Dante's *Divine Comedy.* Examines comic mode as it relates to KAP's fiction.

Pfeffer, Genevieve. "The Characterization and Thematic Use of Old Age in Selected Short Fiction of Katherine Anne Porter, Eudora Welty, and Flannery O'Connor." M.A. thesis, Sam Houston State University, 1973.

Examines old age in the fiction of these writers from the viewpoint of tradition, characterization, motif, structure, and tonal devices.

1974

Cooper, N. M. "From Innocence to Experience in the Fiction of Four Southern Writers." M.A. thesis, Texas Woman's University, 1974.

Includes KAP with Welty, McCullers, and O'Connor to support the theory that the Southern culture, being a unique blending of economic, religious, sociological, and psychological factors, provided the raw material for their artistry.

1975

Stewart, S. A. "Technique and Meaning in Katherine Anne Porter's Short Fiction." M.A. thesis, North Texas State University, 1975.

Attempts to demonstrate a unity of meaning and technique in eight of KAP's stories; maintains that at the core of KAP's work is a delicate balancing of rival considerations designed to show complexity of human relationships. Asserts that the technique is based on KAP's philosophy of life.

Swank, R. A. "Reality and Revelation in the Short Fiction of Katherine Anne Porter." M.A. thesis, North Texas State University, 1975.

Demonstrates that reality and revelation are predominant ideas in KAP's fiction; states that reality as the protagonists perceive it is different from reality as experienced by other characters in the stories; claims that protagonists are better able to face life through the revelation of delusions apparent in the difficulties that involve initiation, subjugation, and alienation.

2. Dissertations

1966

Ledbetter, Nan Wilson Thompson. "The Thumbprint: A Study of People in Katherine Anne Porter's Fiction." *DA*, 28 (1966), 2252A (University of Texas).

Analyzes selected characters from KAP's fiction who are representative of certain themes: initiation, self-delusion, moral definition, and quest.

1967

Waldrip, Louise Dolores Baker. "A Bibliography of the Works of Katherine Anne Porter." *DA*, 27 (1967), 4269A (University of Texas).

Gives a descriptive listing of essays, book reviews, poems, stories, novels, translations, symposiums, introductions or afterwords to works by other authors, and foreign editions of KAP's work from the period 1917–1964.

1974

Pickard, Linda Kay Haskovec. "A Stylo-Linguistic Analysis of Four American Writers." *DAI*, 36 (1974), 6103A (Texas Woman's University).

Examines the "masculine" and "feminine" stylistic characteristics based on lexical and syntactic counts; includes Hemingway's Nick Adams stories, KAP's Miranda stories, J. D. Salinger's *Catcher in the Rye*, and Sylvia Plath's *The Bell Jar*.

1977

Cimarolli, Mary Lou. "Social Criticism as a Structural Factor in Katherine Anne Porter's Fiction." *DAI*, 38 (1977), 6722A (East Texas State University).

Examines KAP's fiction as a commentary on social institutions; includes analysis of KAP's view of the family, war and revolution, the organized church, marriage, and racism.

3. *Symposium Presentations*

1976

DeBellis, Jack. "The Failure of Love in *Ship of Fools*." Katherine Anne Porter Symposium, Howard Payne University, Brownwood, Texas, 10 May 1976.

Givner, Joan. "The Composition of 'The Leaning Tower': A Study of Katherine Anne Porter's Creative Process." Katherine Anne Porter Symposium, Howard Payne University, Brownwood, Texas, 10 May 1976.

James, Almola. "Maria Concepción, Laura and Julia: The Role of Necessity in Rejection." Katherine Anne Porter Symposium, Howard Payne University, Brownwood, Texas, 10 May 1976.

Moore, Andy J. "Regional Imagery: A 'Right Smart' Device in Katherine Anne Porter's 'Noon Wine.'" Katherine Anne Porter Symposium, Howard Payne University, Brownwood, Texas, 10 May 1976.

Unrue, Darlene. "'The Grave' and the Pursuit of Truth." Katherine Anne Porter Symposium, Howard Payne University, Brownwood, Texas, 10 May 1976.

Bass, R. G. "Acceptance and Rejection in 'Flowering Judas.'" Katherine Anne Porter Symposium, Howard Payne University, Brownwood, Texas, 11 May 1976.

Cimarolli, Mary. "Katherine Anne Porter as a Social Critic." Katherine Anne Porter Symposium, Howard Payne University, Brownwood, Texas, 11 May 1976.

Crowder, Elizabeth G. "The Scar and the Tower—The Enemies Without and Within: Katherine Anne Porter's 'The Leaning Tower.'" Katherine Anne Porter Symposium, Howard Payne University, Brownwood, Texas, 11 May 1976.

Fort, Beth. "The Low and Delicious Word Death: Giving Form to Life in 'The Grave.'" Katherine Anne Porter Symposium, Howard Payne University, Brownwood, Texas, 11 May 1976.

Hernandez, Frances. "*Ship of Fools* and *The Winners:* The South American Connection." Katherine Anne Porter Symposium, Howard Payne University, Brownwood, Texas, 11 May 1976.

Hill, R. W. "Emily Dickinson: Dying Again, with Granny Weatherall." Katherine Anne Porter Symposium, Howard Payne University, Brownwood, Texas, 11 May 1976.

Jorgensen, Bruce W. "'The Roar . . . on the Other Side of Silence': Katherine Anne Porter's 'He' as Tragedy." Katherine Anne Porter Symposium, Howard Payne University, Brownwood, Texas, 11 May 1976.

Kiernan, Robert F. "The Forgotten Miranda Stories." Katherine Anne Porter Symposium, Howard Payne University, Brownwood, Texas, 11 May 1976.

Lowe, Alma. "Katherine Anne Porter: The Future Is Now." Katherine Anne Porter Symposium, Howard Payne University, Brownwood, Texas, 11 May 1976.

Wiesenfarth, Joseph. "Katherine Anne Porter and the Destiny of

Man." Katherine Anne Porter Symposium, Howard Payne University, Brownwood, Texas, 11 May 1976.

Givner, Joan. "Katherine Anne Porter's Homecoming." American Studies Association of Texas, Baylor University, Waco, Texas, 13 Nov. 1976.

> Describes KAP's speech at the Katherine Anne Porter Symposium. Analyzes how KAP's expatriate status actually led to her fond memories for and feeling of belonging to Texas after years of inner struggle about her relationship with the state.

1983

Givner, Joan. "Katherine Anne Porter: The Old Order and the New." Conference on Texas Literature, University of Texas, Austin, 24–26 March 1983.

> (Published in *The Texas Literary Tradition: Fiction, Folklore, History;* see section B.2 of this bibliography.)

1984

Brooks, Cleanth. "Romantic Personality, Disciplined Art." Katherine Anne Porter Memorial Lecture, University of Texas at Arlington, 11 April 1984.

Hendrick, George. "Katherine Anne Porter's Texas." Katherine Anne Porter Memorial Lecture, University of Texas at Arlington, 11 April 1984.

Walters, Dorothy. "Female Initiation and Self-Discovery in Porter's Fiction." Katherine Anne Porter Memorial Lecture, University of Texas at Arlington, 11 April 1984.

Givner, Joan. "Katherine Anne Porter: A Writer Disinherited." Texas Women's Literary Tradition: A Conference and Celebration, University of Texas, Austin, 21–22 Sept. 1984.

D. Books about Porter Published in Texas

1967

Emmons, Winfred S. *Katherine Anne Porter: The Regional Stories.* Southwest Writers Series, No. 6. Austin: Steck-Vaughn Company, 1967.

States that much of KAP's best writing is based in Texas; provides an examination of the "regional" stories set in the Southwest and includes "The Old Order," "Old Mortality," "Noon Wine," "He," and "Holiday."

Vann, William H. *The Texas Institute of Letters 1936–1966.* Austin: Encino Press, 1967.

Gives a history of the Texas Institute of Letters; includes KAP as the runner-up to J. Frank Dobie for "Best Texas Book of the Year"; mentions that KAP was the winner of the A. Harris prize for achievement in 1950 and *Ship of Fools* was the winner of the Jesse H. Jones Award for "Best Book of Fiction" in 1962.

1974

Gunn, Drewey Wayne. "'Second Country' Katherine Anne Porter." *American and British Writers in Mexico, 1556–1973.* Austin: University of Texas Press, 1974.

Examines KAP's use of Mexican material in all of her fiction; states that her love for Mexico is revealed in her autobiographical remarks, her fiction, and her nonfiction.

1975

Johns, Erna Victoria Schlemmer. *To Whom It May Concern.* Vol. 1: *The Schlemmers.* Austin: Privately printed, 1975.

Mentions friendship of KAP and Johns, KAP's neighbor in Kyle, Texas.

1982

Greene, A. C. *The 50 Best Books on Texas.* Dallas: Pressworks Publishing, 1982.

Insists that *Pale Horse, Pale Rider* is the best Texas fiction that has ever been written; recalls anecdote of meeting KAP and her insistence that she had never been a newspaper reporter in Dallas; comments that her disavowal of Texas influence was strange since so many of her stories have Texas backgrounds; includes a statement made by KAP to an interviewer after *Pale Horse, Pale Rider* was published that "she could not really imagine 'creating' a story; that everything she had written or would write must be based firmly on a foundation of actual experience."

1983

DeMouy, Jane Krause. *Katherine Anne Porter's Women: The Eye of Her Fiction.* Austin: University of Texas Press, 1983.

Presents a feminist psychological interpretation of KAP's work. Claims that in the canon of Porter's fiction a major theme is the struggle a woman must face, both physically and psychically, between her desire for a conventional life of husband, love, and children, and her freedom of choice. Analyzes fiction from 1922–1934, the Miranda stories from 1935–1936, and *Ship of Fools.*

E. Porter's Correspondence with Texas Writers and the Texas Institute of Letters

Clemons, Walter

Clemons, Walter. Letter to Katherine Anne Porter. New York City, 4 May 1959. 6 pp. TLS. KAP Papers, McL.

Expresses appreciation to KAP for letter of encouragement to Anne Ford of Houghton Mifflin; states that he is sending KAP an inscribed copy of his book; mentions that he will be a writer in residence at Princeton; mentions Horton Foote from Wharton, Texas; includes details of a dinner with Carson McCullers and Horton Foote; expresses admiration for KAP's work.

Clemons, Walter. Letter to Katherine Anne Porter. Houston, Texas, 16 Feb. 1964. 1 p., front and back. TLS. KAP Papers, McL.

Comments on life in Houston, Alley Theater; invites KAP to visit; mentions Larry McMurtry and William Goyen; includes description of the Chekhov production at the Alley Theater; gives plans for the future.

Dobie, J. Frank

Dobie, J. Frank. Letter to Katherine Anne Porter. Austin, Texas, 24 Sept. 1956. 1 p. TLS. KAP Papers, McL.

Extends KAP an invitation to speak at the Texas Institute of Letters; comments on the subject matter; states that KAP may choose her own subject but hopes that she will speak on writing; mentions that the difference between life and literature is often negligible.

Porter, Katherine Anne. Letter to J. Frank Dobie. Southbury, Conn., 3 Oct. 1956. 1 p. TLS, HW note on side. KAP Papers, McL (CC); KAP Papers, HRC (original).

Replies to Dobie's invitation to speak at Texas Institute of Letters; requests fee of $250 plus expenses; comments on her writing.

Dobie, J. Frank. Letter to Katherine Anne Porter. Austin, Texas, 16 Oct. 1956. 1 p. TLS. KAP Papers, HRC (CC); KAP Papers, McL (original).

Includes additional invitation to speak at SMU at the same time as KAP's appearance before Texas Institute of Letters; mentions Lon Tinkle of SMU and the *Dallas Morning News.*

Dobie, J. Frank. Letter to Katherine Anne Porter. Austin, Texas, 23 Oct. 1956. 1 p. TLS. KAP Papers, HRC (CC); KAP Papers, McL (original).

Extends invitation for KAP to speak not only for Texas Institute of Letters and SMU but also at North Texas State University; states that fee schedule will be $150 per appearance plus $250 from TIL.

Porter, Katherine Anne. Letter to J. Frank Dobie. Southbury, Conn., 21 Nov. 1956. 1 p. TLS. KAP Papers, McL (CC); KAP Papers, HRC (original).

Regrets that she will not be able to make the Texas tour because of deadline from her publisher and low speaking fees in Texas.

Dobie, J. Frank. Letter to Katherine Anne Porter. Austin, Texas, 7 Dec. 1956. 1 p. TLS. KAP Papers, HRC (CC); KAP Papers, McL (original).

Acknowledges KAP's refusal to come to Texas to speak; includes a statement about the attitude of colleges toward speakers.

Goyen, William

(All entries are located in the Katherine Anne Porter Papers, Mc-Keldin Library, Maryland.)

Porter, Katherine Anne. Letter to William Goyen. New York City, 7 June 1951. 4 pp. TL, n. sig., last p. unfinished.

Comments on relationship with Goyen.

Porter, Katherine Anne. Letter to William Goyen. New York City, 8 June 1951. 1/2 p. TL, CC, n. sig.

Comments on relationship with Goyen; expresses distaste for people who always want something from her.

Porter, Katherine Anne. Letter to William Goyen. New York City, 8 June 1951. 1/2 p. TL, n. sig.

Expresses feelings for Goyen.

Porter, Katherine Anne. Letter to William Goyen. New York City, 6 Jul. 1951. 1 p., front and back. TL, n. sig., HW penciled corr.

Expresses frustration over her relationship with Goyen; gives a long commentary on Goyen-KAP relationship.

Porter, Katherine Anne. Letter to William Goyen. New York City, 14 Jul. 1951. 2 pp. TL, HW corr., n. sig.

States that she is returning to Paris to try to put together her life; expresses dislike for people who try to use her; gives long statement on her need to be loved and her abhorrence of being used.

Porter, Katherine Anne. Letter to William Goyen. New York City, Bastille Day 1951. 1 p., front and back. TLS, HW corr.

Discusses book that she had lost and how she found it.

Porter, Katherine Anne. Letter to William Goyen. New York City, 16 Jul. 1951. 1 p., front and back. TL, n. sig.

States her wishes to end relationship with Goyen; comments on their friendship.

Porter, Katherine Anne. Letter to William Goyen. New York City, 1 Aug. 1951. 1 p. TL, n. sig., HW penciled corr., unfinished.

Comments on Goyen's *A Shape of Light.*

Porter, Katherine Anne. Letter to William Goyen. New York City, 17 Aug. 1951. 2 1/2 pp. TL, CC, n. sig.

Comments on Icarus; writes about her philosophy of life, the fall of man; gives similarities in the thoughts of KAP and Goyen; reminisces about times together.

Goyen, William. Card to Katherine Anne Porter. New York City, Easter 1952. 1 p. ALS.

Comments on relationship between KAP and Goyen.

Porter, Katherine Anne. Letter to William Goyen. N. add., 12 Apr. 1952. 1 p. TLS, penciled note.

Comments on relationship of KAP and William Goyen.

Goyen, William. Letter to Katherine Anne Porter. New York City, 23 May 1952. 1 p., front and back. ALS.

Comments on KAP in Paris; expresses desire for news from Paris; mentions trip to see his mother.

Porter, Katherine Anne. Letter to William Goyen. Paris, France, 2 June 1952. 4 pp. TLS, CC.

Describes life in Paris.

Goyen, William. Letter to Katherine Anne Porter. New York City, 6 June 1952. 1 p., front and back. TLS.

Mentions the KAP and Goyen relationship; includes details of life in New York City.

Porter, Katherine Anne. Letter to William Goyen. Paris, France, 11 June 1952. 2 pp. TLS, CC.

States that she will not be moving back to New York; gives details of adventures in France and plans for future travel.

Goyen, William. Letter to Katherine Anne Porter. New York City, 3 Jul., n. yr. 1 p., front and back. TLS.

States that he cannot come to Paris to see KAP as planned; mentions he has lost his passport; writes about Goyen-KAP relationship.

Porter, Katherine Anne. Letter to William Goyen. Paris, France, 11 Jul. 1952. 1 p., front and back. TLS, CC.

Expresses disappointment that Goyen cannot join her in Paris; gives details of travel plans; mentions homes in Paris.

Porter, Katherine Anne. Letter to William Goyen. New York City, 20 Jul., n. yr. 2 pp. TL, n. sig.

Complains about sexual perversion and attitudes toward women in current books.

Goyen, William. Letter to Katherine Anne Porter. Chicago, Ill., 29 Dec., n. yr. 1 p. ALS, HW penciled corr. by KAP.

Gives the details of meeting planned for 4 Jan., not 2 Jan.

Goyen, William. Letter to Katherine Anne Porter. New York City, n.d., 1952. 1 p., front and back. ALS.

Thanks KAP for a book; includes personal details.

Porter, Katherine Anne. Letter to William Goyen. Paris, France, n.d. 2 pp. TL, CC, n. sig.

Gives a long commentary on Goyen; mentions story in the *San Antonio Express;* discusses future plans.

Hudson, Wilson M.

   Hudson, Wilson M. Letter to Katherine Anne Porter. N. add.,
   20 June 1961. 1 p. TLS. KAP Papers, McL.

     Informs KAP that she has been elected a member of the Texas In-
     stitute of Letters.

Humphrey, William

   (All entries are located in the Katherine Anne Porter Papers, Mc-
   Keldin Library, University of Maryland.)

   Humphrey, William. Letter to Katherine Anne Porter. Annan-
   dale-on-Hudson, N.Y. (Bard College), 20 Sept. 1950. 1 p. TLS.

     Invites KAP to speak at Bard College.

   Porter, Katherine Anne. Letter to William Humphrey. New York
   City, 26 Sept. 1950. 2 pp. TL, CC, HW corr., n. sig.

     Accepts invitation to Bard College; writes of her illness and her ad-
     miration for Humphrey's work.

   Humphrey, William. Letter to Katherine Anne Porter. N. add.,
   28 Sept. 1950. 3 pp. TLS, HW corr.

     Praises KAP's work. States that through his reading of her work he
     found what he wanted to do as a profession. Calls KAP a great
     teacher. Gives details of arrangements for KAP's visit to Bard
     College.

   Porter, Katherine Anne. Letter to William Humphrey. New York
   City, 30 Sept. 1950. 2 pp. TLS, CC.

     Writes concerning the arrangements for travel to Bard College; ex-
     presses praise for Humphrey's work and states that she is pleased to
     have provided an example for him.

   Porter, Katherine Anne. Letter to William Humphrey. New York
   City, 8 Oct. 1950. 1 p. TLS.

     Writes regarding dinner invitation for Humphrey and William
     Goyen on Sunday, October 14; includes a statement about Texas;
     states that she has never felt any affection for Texas and that she left
     Texas as early in her life as possible. Mentions that Texas scholars
     have tried to include her in their ranks only in the last few years.
     Comments that she has met fascinating Texans outside of Texas but
     that she never believed a true artist could come from Texas.

Humphrey, William. Letter to Katherine Anne Porter. N. add., n.d., 1950. 1 p. TLS, HW corr.

Accepts dinner invitation with KAP.

Humphrey, William. Letter to Katherine Anne Porter. N. add., 19 Oct. 1950. 1 p. TLS.

Thanks KAP for the evening spent with her; writes lavish praise to her.

Porter, Katherine Anne. Letter to William Humphrey. New York City, 21 Oct. 1950. 1 p. TLS, CC.

Apologizes for misunderstanding *The Fauve* by Humphrey.

Humphrey, William. Letter to Katherine Anne Porter. Bard College, N.Y., 30 Nov. 1950. 1 p. TLS.

Gives the train schedule from New York to Bard College for KAP's lecture.

Humphrey, William. Letter to Katherine Anne Porter. N. add., n.d., 1950. 1 p. TLS, HW corr.

Gives more details of December 13 visit of KAP to Bard College; wants her suggestions on unpublished material he is sending KAP; requests a personal visit.

Porter, Katherine Anne. Letter to William Humphrey. New York City, Twelfth Night 1951. 2 pp. TL, CC, n. sig., unfinished.

Writes of KAP's illness; includes commentary on universities that require publication from faculty members.

Humphrey, William. Letter to Katherine Anne Porter. N. add., 29 Dec. 1951. 1 p. ALS.

Inquires about KAP's health.

Humphrey, William. Letter to Katherine Anne Porter. N. add., n.d., 1951. 1 p. TLS.

Comments on the life of a professor, the frustrations of the job; states that the only compensation of teaching is that he is paid to read.

Humphrey, William. Letter to Katherine Anne Porter. Rhinebeck, N.Y., 3 Jan. 1958. 1 p. ALS.

Requests an appointment for a visit.

Porter, Katherine Anne. Letter to William Humphrey. Connecticut, 12 Jan. 1958. 3 1/2 pp. TLS, CC, HW corr.

Writes of her frustrations as a writer; resents the pulls and pressures; states that she has had a series of crises; comments on the progress of her novel and mentions Humphrey's novel; includes family news.

Humphrey, William. Letter to Katherine Anne Porter. New York, 15 Jan. 1958. 1 p. TLS, HW corr.

Expresses appreciation for KAP's comments on his work.

Porter, Katherine Anne. Letter to William Humphrey. Connecticut, St. Valentine's Day 1958. 1 p., front and back. TLS, CC.

Praises Humphrey's *Home from the Hill;* comments on her slow progress on *Ship of Fools.*

Humphrey, William. Letter to Katherine Anne Porter. New York, 28 Feb. 1958. 2 pp. TLS.

Writes of the pleasure over the success of his book; encourages KAP to find the patience to finish her book.

Humphrey, William. Letter to Katherine Anne Porter. Rhinebeck, N.Y., 31 May 1958. 1 p. TLS.

Gives details of plans for Humphrey and his wife to leave for Britain.

Porter, Katherine Anne. Letter to William Humphrey. Connecticut, 5 June 1958. 1 p. TLS, CC.

Expresses pleasure over Humphrey's plans; writes that the novel is almost finished; gives plans to leave Connecticut and go to University of Virginia and then to Washington and Lee University.

Humphrey, William. Letter to Katherine Anne Porter. Lexington, Va., 11 Jan. 1963. 1 p. TLS.

Gives KAP the details of his work and life.

Porter, Katherine Anne. Letter to William Humphrey. Washington, D.C., 15 Jan. 1964. 1 p., front and back. TLS, CC.

Gives Humphrey the details of her life and work; mentions *Ship of Fools'* reception by critics; states that she is grateful for Humphrey's praise.

Porter, Katherine Anne. Letter to William Humphrey. Washington, D.C., 2 Mar. 1965. 2 pp. TL, CC, T sig.

Praises Humphrey's *The Ordways;* asks Humphrey to be the executor of her will if Glenway Wescott does not outlive KAP.

Humphrey, William. Letter to Katherine Anne Porter. Rome, Italy, 25 Mar. 1965. 1 p. ALS.

Accepts happily to act as KAP's executor.

Porter, Katherine Anne. Letter to William Humphrey. Washington, D.C., 28 Mar. 1965. 1 p. TLS, CC.

Thanks Humphrey for agreeing to act as her executor; praises *The Ordways.*

Humphrey, William. Letter to Katherine Anne Porter. Rome, Italy, 16 Apr. 1965. 1 p. ALS.

Regrets that he cannot visit KAP; states that he feels that he must visit relatives and his editor; includes plans for moving to New York.

Porter, Katherine Anne. Letter to William Humphrey. Washington, D.C., 28 Apr. 1965. 1 p. TL, CC, T sig.

Mentions visit of Wescott and the executorship of KAP's will; states that she plans to remain in Washington, D.C.; comments on job opportunity at Colorado State University.

Humphrey, William. Letter to Katherine Anne Porter. Poughkeepsie, N.Y., 4 May 1965. 1 p. ALS.

Describes living arrangements in New York.

Humphrey, William. Letter to Katherine Anne Porter. Poughkeepsie, N.Y., 21 May 1965. 1 p. TLS.

Writes of discouragement over the housing situation in New York; requests the names of magazines *Ship of Fools* excerpts have appeared in.

Humphrey, William. Letter to Katherine Anne Porter. Poughkeepsie, N.Y., 24 May 1965. 1 p. TLS.

Gives KAP an update on his living and working situation; mentions going to Massachusetts Institute of Technology for an interview; comments on the housing situation.

Porter, Katherine Anne. Letter to William Humphrey. Washington, D.C., 24 May 1965. 1 p. TLS, CC.

Writes about "St. Augustine and the Bullfight" and "Defense of Circe"; includes a long statement about Circe and why KAP wrote the essay; discusses housing problems and money problems.

Porter, Katherine Anne. Letter to William Humphrey. Washington, D.C., 11 June 1965. 1 p. TL, CC, n. sig.

Comments on "A Wreath for the Game Keeper" and states that she finds D. H. Lawrence's view of sex nauseating; writes more about Circe; comments that the tax structure is draining her money away.

Humphrey, William. Letter to Katherine Anne Porter. N. add., 21 June 1965. 1 p. ALS.

Requests a visit with KAP; compliments "The Wooden Umbrella"; states that the article of KAP's is a perfect joy.

Porter, Katherine Anne. Letter to William Humphrey. Washington, D.C., 5 Jul. 1965. 1 p. TLS, HW telephone number.

Agrees to meet with Humphrey and his wife; states that she is anxious for a visit.

Humphrey, William. Letter to Katherine Anne Porter. Cambridge, Mass., 22 Sept. 1965. 1 p. TLS.

Thanks KAP for the visit with her; states that he is looking for a library to house the KAP Papers but not Harvard because women are not allowed in the library.

Humphrey, William. Letter to Katherine Anne Porter. Cambridge, Mass., 15 Dec. 1965. 1 p. ALS.

Describes his life and work; states that he is returning a borrowed book.

Humphrey, William. Letter to Katherine Anne Porter. N. add., n.d. 1 p. ALS.

Expresses concern for KAP's health.

Humphrey, William. Letter to Katherine Anne Porter. N. add., n.d. 3 pp. TLS, HW corr. and postscript.

Expounds his ideas on teaching; states that he is grateful for his job and that there is actually a lack of pressure; wants to relieve KAP of fears that he is under too much pressure.

Humphrey, William. Letter to Katherine Anne Porter. N. add., 2 Apr., n. yr. 1 p. TLS.

Expresses concern for KAP's health.

Humphrey, William. Letter to Katherine Anne Porter. N. add., n.d. 1 p. ALS.

Suggests that KAP send the excerpts of the Cotton Mather manuscript to the *Quarterly Review of Literature* because the editor had expressed an interest in it.

Perry, George Sessions

Porter, Katherine Anne. Letter to George Sessions Perry. Ballston Spa, N.Y., 5 Feb. 1943 (envelope dated 6 Feb. 1943). 1/2 p. TLS. KAP Papers, HRC.

Refuses to give permission to reprint "Maria Concepción"; comments that she is willing to be regarded as a Texas writer although she considers herself more Southern than Southwestern. Mentions other places she has lived outside of Texas. States that the scenes of "Maria Concepción" were set about ten miles outside of Mexico City, but that "Noon Wine," "Old Mortality," and "He" were all set between San Marcos and Austin, Texas.

F. PORTER'S CORRESPONDENCE WITH THE UNIVERSITY OF TEXAS.

Allen, Winnie

Allen, Winnie. Letter to Katherine Anne Porter. Austin, Texas, 4 June 1953. 1 p. TLS. KAP Papers, McL.

Requests a KAP manuscript for the Barker Texas History Center collection. (Winnie Allen is an archivist with the University of Texas at Austin.)

Porter, Katherine Anne. Letter to Miss Winnie Allen. New York City, 10 June 1953. 1 p. TLS, CC, HW corr. and notes. KAP Papers, McL.

Mentions that "Old Mortality" is set between San Marcos and Austin in Hays County; states that she sent Miss Allen her typewritten, hand-corrected draft of "Old Mortality" but that the manuscript has probably been lost; includes comments about the University of Texas, states that she understands all University of Texas funds are spent for buildings and none for salaries; mentions that she will not give anything that is negotiable to the University of Texas.

Benavides, Magdalena

Benavides, Magdalena. Letter to Katherine Anne Porter. N. add., 24 Jul. 1959. 1 p. TL, T. sig., photocopy. KAP Papers. BTHC.

Sends KAP the galley proofs for the *Ship of Fools* excerpt in *Texas Quarterly;* requests return of the corrected galley proofs by August 5 or the editorial staff will make the necessary changes.

Blanchard, Charles B.

Blanchard, Charles B. Letter to the Copyright Department, *Texas Quarterly.* Boston, Mass., 14 Aug. 1961. 1 p. TLS, photocopy. KAP Papers, BTHC.

Requests information about the publication of an excerpt of *Ship of Fools* in the *Texas Quarterly;* requests the assignment of copyright on the excerpt.

Boatright, Mody

Boatright, Mody. Letter to Katherine Anne Porter. Austin, Texas, 19 Dec. 1958. 1 p. TL, T sig. KAP Papers, BTHC (CC); KAP Papers, McL (original).

Offers KAP a position as visiting professor at the University of Texas at a salary of $6,000; states the terms of her position.

Porter, Katherine Anne. Letter to Mody Boatright. Charlottesville, Va., 26 Dec. 1958. 1 p. TLS, HW corr. KAP Papers, McL (CC); KAP Papers, BTHC (original).

Accepts position on the staff of the University of Texas for the fall semester of 1959; comments that she is awed by the university's decision to name the Library Center for her; states that the library is the nicest honor she has ever received; offers to the library as a token of her appreciation her entire literary estate; comments that her estate consists of papers, manuscripts, notes, correspondence, photographs, and books. States that her offer is only provisional; requests that Boatright tell her how and to whom to make the offer. Mentions making a new will.

Boatright, Mody. Letter to Katherine Anne Porter. Austin, Texas, 14 Apr. 1959. 1 p. TL, T. sig. KAP Papers, BTHC (CC); KAP Papers, McL (original).

Gives KAP her schedule for fall classes: "Short Story Workshop," Mon., Wed., Fri. at 10:00; "The Modern Short Story," Tues., Thurs., Sat. at 9:00. Includes details about class size, etc., and requests return of forms.

Porter, Katherine Anne. Letter to Mody Boatright. Lexington, Va., 29 Apr. 1959. 2½ pp. TLS. KAP Papers, McL (CC); KAP Papers, BTHC (original).

Mentions the difficulty she has with filling out forms; requests a new set of biographical data sheets; insists on Robert Penn Warren's and Cleanth Brooks's *Understanding Fiction* as text for her classes; includes plans for her arrival in Austin in August.

Boatright, Mody. Letter to Katherine Anne Porter. Austin, Texas, May, 1959. 1 p. TL, T. sig. KAP Papers, BTHC (CC); KAP Papers, McL (original).

Comments about the biographical data sheet sent to KAP from the University of Texas.

Porter, Katherine Anne. Letter to Mody Boatright. Lexington, Va., 19 May 1959. 1 p. ALS. KAP Papers, BTHC.

States she is preparing to move to Washington, D.C., and will tape-record her stories for the Library of Congress Division of the Blind; requests that he write to her in care of her publisher.

Porter, Katherine Anne. Letter to Mody Boatright. N. add., n.d. 2 pp. TL, T. sig., photocopy; original also with HW date, 25 May 1959. KAP Papers, BTHC.

States reason she must resign from her commitment to the University of Texas: Ford Foundation will not allow her to receive other compensation during the time of her grant. Mentions that she will be able to give an occasional reading; comments that she was scheduled for Ewing Lecture at UCLA but lost her voice during the airplane trip; questions Boatright about the plans for the Library Center.

Boatright, Mody. Letter to J. A. Burdine (College of Arts and Sciences, University of Texas). Austin, Texas, 28 May 1959. 1 p. TL, CC, T. sig. KAP Papers, BTHC.

States that KAP will not be able to be a writer in residence at the University of Texas because of the Ford Foundation grant, recommends that KAP be invited as a visiting professor in English for the next academic year and includes the conditions of the future assignment.

Boatright, Mody. Letter to Katherine Anne Porter. Austin, Texas, 29 May 1959. 1 p. TL, T. sig. KAP Papers, BTHC (CC); KAP Papers, McL (original).

Expresses regret that KAP will not be on the staff at the University of Texas; allows for possible visiting professorship in the future.

Porter, Katherine Anne. Letter to Mody Boatright. Washington, D.C., 16 June 1959. 1 p. TLS. KAP Papers, McL (CC); KAP Papers, BTHC (original).

Accepts the offer of visiting professorship without salaries or duties, states that she will come to Austin to look for a house. Expresses thoughts on Texas; mentions that her mother is buried at Indian Creek and her grandmother at Kyle.

Boatright, Mody. Letter to Katherine Anne Porter. N. add., 1 Jul. 1959. 1 p. TL, CC, T. sig. KAP Papers, BTHC.

Expresses pleasure that KAP is coming to work at the University of Texas; comments on the number of invitations for speaking engagements KAP has already received; states that he will contribute his copy of June 1937 *Story* to the Katherine Anne Porter Room.

Porter, Katherine Anne. Letter to Mody Boatright. Washington, D.C., 9 Aug. 1959. 1 p. TLS, HW corr. KAP Papers, McL (CC); KAP Papers, BTHC (original).

Announces plans to remain in Washington, D.C., instead of moving to Austin; states that she has accepted a Ford Foundation grant and that she needs solitude to work.

Boatright, Mody. Letter to Katherine Anne Porter. N. add., 28 Aug. 1959. 1 p. TL, T. sig. KAP Papers, BTHC (CC); KAP Papers, McL (original).

Expresses regret that KAP will not be at the University of Texas but understands that her writing and solitude are of primary importance.

Porter, Katherine Anne. Postcard to Mody Boatright. Washington, D.C., 15 Oct. 1959. ALS. KAP Papers, BTHC.

Sends Boatright her new address.

Porter, Katherine Anne. Letter to Mody Boatright. Washington, D.C., 1 Jan. 1964. 1 p. TLS, CC. KAP Papers, McL.

Inquires about interview on her childhood and family; writes that she had even seen the proofs of the interview, but she has not heard about the final published form; mentions plans to be in Dallas in February.

Boatright, Mody. Letter to Katherine Anne Porter. Austin, Texas, 8 Jan. 1964. 1 p. TLS. KAP Papers, McL.

States that the interview with KAP about her childhood and family is to be published in a special "Katherine Anne Porter Issue" of the *Texas Observer;* includes a comment that the editor of the *Observer,* Ronnie Dugger, had delayed publication of the issue because of the presidential assassination.

Porter, Katherine Anne. Letter to Mody Boatright. N. add., n.d. 2 pp. TLS, CC. KAP Papers, McL.

States that she will not be able to accept the teaching position at the University of Texas at Austin because of the restrictions of the Ford Foundation grant; mentions more lucrative teaching offers from other universities; states that she feels she cannot refuse the offer from the Ford Foundation of being able to work without teaching responsibilities.

Boatright, Mody. Memo to Harry Ransom. University of Texas, Austin, Texas, n.d. 1 p. ALS, HW: postscript from Marguerite Carlson. KAP Papers, BTHC.

Requests that Ransom write KAP concerning her book collection; states that KAP is anxious to leave her materials to the Porter Collection.

Dockery, Faye

Dockery, Faye. Letter to Katherine Anne Porter. Austin, Texas, 19 Aug. 1959. 1 p. TLS. KAP Papers, McL.

Requests that KAP fill out forms to receive payment from the University of Texas Press.

Porter, Katherine Anne. Letter to Faye Dockery. Washington, D.C., 4 Dec. 1959. 1 p. TLS, CC. KAP Papers, McL.

Informs Dockery that she has not received $500 fee for *Ship of Fools* excerpt published in *Texas Quarterly;* requests Dockery to see that the money is remitted.

Handy, William

Handy, William. Letter to Katherine Anne Porter. Austin, Texas, 8 Oct. 1958. 1 p. TLS. KAP Papers, McL.

Extends an invitation to KAP to participate in the University of Texas Program in Criticism; mentions fee of $600 to cover expenses and the honorarium.

Porter, Katherine Anne. Letter to William Handy. Charlottesville, Va., 12 Oct. 1958. 2 pp. ALS. KAP Papers, BTHC.

Encloses curriculum vitae information and photograph; gives plans
to be at Washington and Lee University in the spring; states that she
will read her essay "'Noon Wine': The Sources," and mentions that
this will be her first trip to Texas since 1936; inquires about the details of her reading performances and requests certain considerations.

Porter, Katherine Anne. Letter to William Handy. Charlottesville,
Va., 16 Oct. 1958. 1 p. TLS. KAP Papers, BTHC (photocopy);
KAP Papers, HRC (original).

Writes details of her arrival in Austin.

Handy, William. Letter to Katherine Anne Porter. Austin, Texas,
31 Oct. 1958. 2 pp. ALS. KAP Papers, BTHC (photocopy); KAP
Papers, McL (original).

Informs KAP that she will be invited to teach at the University of
Texas for one semester during the 1959–1960 school year. States that
members of the faculty and student body are most enthusiastic about
KAP coming to Texas; mentions that everyone in the university from
Dr. Ransom to the undergraduate students felt that she was the best
visiting lecturer the University of Texas had ever had.

Porter, Katherine Anne. Letter to William Handy. Charlottesville, Va., 31 Oct. 1958. 1 p. TLS, HW corr., photocopy. KAP
Papers, BTHC.

Expresses appreciation for the copies of the *Texas Quarterly;* mentions
Deirdre Handy's thesis on KAP; comments on her visit to Texas and
her displeasure about the picture in the newspaper; states she has
visited Oklahoma.

Handy, William. Letter to Katherine Anne Porter. Austin, Texas,
18 June 1959. 1 p. ALS. KAP Papers, McL.

Comments on KAP's decision to move to Texas.

Porter, Katherine Anne. Letter to William Handy. Washington,
D.C., 30 June 1959. 2 1/2 pp. TLS, HW corr. KAP Papers, McL
(CC); KAP Papers, BTHC (photocopy); KAP Papers, HRC
(original).

States feelings about being invited to be a writer in residence; mentions that she will not have a salary or duties but merely an office;
writes about yearning for privacy and wanting a house.

Handy, William. Letter to Katherine Anne Porter. Austin, Texas, 6 Aug. 1959. 2 pp. ALS. KAP Papers, McL.

Comments on finding a suitable house for KAP when she moves to Texas; mentions the KAP library; states that the Katherine Anne Porter Library in the Academic Center will begin to take shape by the following spring.

Porter, Katherine Anne. Letter to William Handy. Washington, D.C., 9 Aug. 1959. 1 p. TLS. KAP Papers, McL (CC); KAP Papers, HRC (original).

States that she will not be coming to Texas as a writer in residence at the University of Texas; mentions her dream of having a house and a garden with pomegranates and figs.

Handy, William. Letter to Katherine Anne Porter. Austin, Texas, 10 Sept. 1959. 1 p. TLS. KAP Papers, McL.

Expresses regret that KAP will not be moving to Texas.

Porter, Katherine Anne. Postcard to William Handy. Washington, D.C., 15 Oct. 1959. ALS. KAP Papers, BTHC.

Sends Handy her new address.

Porter, Katherine Anne. Letter to William Handy. Charlottesville, Va., 31 Oct. 1959. 1 p. TLS, CC. KAP Papers, McL.

Thanks Handy for the copy of his wife's thesis on KAP's work.

Handy, William. Letter to Katherine Anne Porter. Austin, Texas, 5 Nov. 1959. 1 p. ALS. KAP Papers, McL.

Seeks clarification of details concerning delay of check to KAP and the two back issues of *Texas Quarterly* KAP had requested.

Porter, Katherine Anne. Letter to William Handy. Washington, D.C., n.d. 1 p., front and back. TLS, CC. KAP Papers, McL.

Requests check from the *Texas Quarterly* and also two back issues of the *Texas Quarterly* that she is missing from her collection.

Porter, Katherine Anne. Letter to William J. Handy. Washington, D.C., n.d. 2 pp. TLS. KAP Papers, BTHC.

Writes about the two missing copies of the *Texas Quarterly* and the forms that she has signed concerning remuneration for the *Ship of Fools* excerpt; asks Handy to check on the situation; comments on Louis Rubin's *No Place on Earth;* mentions Miss Ellen, Cabell's "Let

Me Lie"; requests that Handy find the two missing copies of the *Texas Quarterly.*

Handy, Mrs. William

Porter, Katherine Anne. Letter to Mrs. William Handy. Charlottesville, Va., 23 Jan. 1959. 2 pp. TLS, HW corr. and postscript. KAP Papers, BTHC (photocopy); KAP Papers, HRC (original).

Comments on the essay Mrs. Handy wrote; mentions the problems of life that she (KAP) faces.

Hudspeth, Frances

Hudspeth, Frances. Letter to Katherine Anne Porter. Austin, Texas, 24 Oct. 1958. 1 p. TLS. KAP Papers, McL (original); KAP Papers, BTHC (photocopy).

Requests permission to publish a portion of *Ship of Fools* in the *Texas Quarterly.*

Porter, Katherine Anne. Letter to Frances Hudspeth. Charlottesville, Va., All Saints Eve 1958. 1 p. TLS, HW corr. KAP Papers, BTHC.

Comments on the sequences of *Ship of Fools;* states that none of it has been published; accepts a stipend of $500; mentions enjoyment of her visit to the University of Texas; requests information about her missing copy of the *Yale Review* that she thinks she left at Frank Lyell's home.

Porter, Katherine Anne. Letter to Frances Hudspeth. Charlottesville, Va., n.d., 1958. 1 p. TLS, CC. KAP Papers, McL.

States that she is sending Hudspeth a segment of *Ship of Fools;* comments on the Jewish episodes in *Ship of Fools;* accepts a $500 stipend.

Hudspeth, Frances. Letter to Katherine Anne Porter. Austin, Texas, 23 Feb. 1959. 1 p. TL, T sig. KAP Papers, McL (original); KAP Papers, BTHC (photocopy).

Writes that she is not sending KAP the original manuscript of *Ship of Fools* but a typescript for KAP's corrections; requests information about the publication date; mentions plans for the new library.

Porter, Katherine Anne. Letter to Frances Hudspeth. Lexington, Va., 1 Mar. 1959. 2 pp. TLS, HW corr. and postscript. KAP Papers, McL (CC); KAP Papers, BTHC (photocopy).

Comments on the decision of the editorial board of the *Texas Quarterly* regarding passages from *Ship of Fools;* gives a long statement on freedom of thought; inquires about information on the Katherine Anne Porter Library; states that she is most anxious for any data on her library; mentions that she wishes to examine the drawings and that she plans to be buried in the floor of the library. States that she would rather have a library than any prize including the Nobel. Calls herself totally in love with her library.

Porter, Katherine Anne. Letter to Frances Hudspeth. Lexington, Va., 25 May 1959. 1 p. TLS, CC. KAP Papers, McL.

Inquires if Hudspeth received the corrected manuscript for *Ship of Fools* segment that is to be published in the *Texas Quarterly.*

Lyell, Frank

Lyell, Frank. Letter to Katherine Anne Porter. Austin, Texas, 17 Oct. 1958. 1 p., front and back. ALS. KAP Papers, McL.

Writes of the excitement over the forthcoming KAP visit to Austin; states that he plans to meet her at the airport.

Porter, Katherine Anne. Letter to Frank Lyell. Charlottesville, Va., 1 Jan. 1959. 1 p. TLS, HW corr. KAP Papers, BTHC.

Writes about future travel and teaching positions; gives plans to be in Austin by September; mentions the new Katherine Anne Porter Library. Comments that all she ever wanted was glory and that the new library makes her very happy. Mentions culture in Texas. Remembers that as a child she heard every famous musician who traveled to her part of Texas. Comments that few people from the North believe her because they think that Texas is only cowboys and oilmen.

Lyell, Frank. Memorandum to the Vice-President and President of the University of Texas. Austin, Texas (Department of English, University of Texas), 26 May 1960. 2 pp., front and back. ALS. KAP Papers, BTHC.

Questions what part of the undergraduate library is to be named for KAP; mentions Marcella Winslow, an artist in Washington, D.C., who has a portrait of KAP that might be suitable for the Katherine Anne Porter Library; requests instructions on whether he should examine the portrait.

Meriwether, James

Meriwether, James. Letter to Katherine Anne Porter. Austin, Texas, 5 Feb. 1959. 1 p. TLS. KAP Papers, McL.

Requests permission to transcribe KAP's television interview about Faulkner and use it in an anthology of *Writers on Faulkner.*

Porter, Katherine Anne. Letter to James Meriwether. Lexington, Va., 9 Feb. 1959. 1 p. TLS, CC, HW corr. KAP Papers, McL.

Gives permission to Meriwether to use the Faulkner transcription; writes about her immense frustration, feels pulled by people and cannot finish her work because of the necessity of earning a living on the lecture tour.

Meriwether, James. Letter to Katherine Anne Porter. N. add., 17 Apr. 1959. 1 p. TLS. KAP Papers, McL.

Expresses appreciation for allowing him to use the transcription; includes a copy of the transcription for KAP to emend.

Porter, Katherine Anne. Letter to James Meriwether. Lexington, Va., 29 Apr. 1959. 2 1/2 pp. TLS, CC, HW corr. KAP Papers, McL.

Accepts Meriwether's transcription correction; expresses feeling that text is not exactly as she had intended; mentions schedule in Virginia; comments on the pleasure of being in Texas and inquires about library.

Ransom, Harry

Ransom, Harry. Letter to Katherine Anne Porter. Austin, Texas, 7 Nov. 1958. 1 p. TLS. KAP Papers, BTHC (CC); KAP Papers, McL (original).

Compliments KAP on her visit to Austin; announces that the administration has voted to establish the Katherine Anne Porter Library in the Library Center that is being built on the Austin campus; encourages KAP to accept the visiting professorship in the Department of English the next year.

Porter, Katherine Anne. Letter to Harry Ransom. Charlottesville, Va., 16 Nov. 1958. 2 pp. TLS. KAP Papers, McL (CC); KAP Papers, BTHC (original).

Describes her traveling plans; expresses excitement over the library that is to be named for her at the University of Texas; states that she is extremely excited over the library; calls the proposed library exactly what she would have wanted if she could have chosen a memorial for her life. States that she still plans to come as a visiting professor and announces that she plans to live permanently in Texas. Includes thoughts on Ima Hogg's father; calls him a friend of Grandmother Porter's; remembers him sitting in her grandmother's front room drinking cold buttermilk and smiling agreeably at her grandmother. States that they looked like cronies but that neither her grandmother nor Governor Hogg would have approved of such a description.

Porter, Katherine Anne. Letter to Harry Ransom. Charlottesville, Va., 1 Jan. 1959. 1 p. TLS, HW corr. KAP Papers, McL (CC); KAP Papers, BTHC (original).

Comments on health problems; states that she is to go to Washington and Lee University as a visiting professor; includes long statement about the Katherine Anne Porter Library; inquires about what she should do about her library between the announcement of its naming and the laying of the cornerstone; states that she does not plan to have any part in the publicity about the library; calls the naming of her library a great event and states that she wants to conduct herself in the most proper way and not do anything inappropriate; requests instructions or advice about every aspect of the naming of the library.

Ransom, Harry. Letter to Katherine Anne Porter. Austin, Texas, 27 May 1959. 1 p. TL, CC., T. sig. KAP Papers, BTHC (CC); KAP Papers, McL (original).

Expresses disappointment that KAP cannot be at the University of Texas; extends a standing invitation to come to Texas; includes plans for the Academic Center and the Katherine Anne Porter Library; comments that he anticipates three years until completion; states that plans for the Katherine Anne Porter Library and the Academic Center are steadily progressing.

Ransom, Harry. Letter to J. Alton Burdine (College of Arts and Sciences, University of Texas). Austin, Texas, 27 May 1959. 1 p. TL, CC, T. sig. KAP Papers, BTHC.

States that KAP will not be at the University of Texas for the fall semester of 1959.

Ransom, Harry. Letter to Katherine Anne Porter. Austin, Texas, 4 June 1959. 1 p. TLS. KAP Papers, BTHC (CC); KAP Papers, McL (original).

Expresses regret that KAP will not be in Texas; offers to schedule a lecture conference for her at her convenience; inquires about the

KAP papers; suggests that she allow him to present some ideas about the disposition of the Porter Collection.

Porter, Katherine Anne. Letter to Harry Ransom. Washington, D.C., 16 June 1959. 2 pp. TLS, HW corr. KAP Papers, McL (CC); KAP Papers, BTHC (original).

Writes about her plans to return to Texas; states that she is definitely planning to move back to Texas and to remain there the rest of her life; refutes Thomas Wolfe's statement that you can't go home again and says that home is the only place to go. Comments on the personal material she plans to bring to Texas and makes suggestions regarding the disposition of her material; states that several universities have been interested in her collection; comments that she wants to be actively involved in its arrangement; suggests that the university pay her salary as curator of her collection for no less than three years and that she have a trained assistant to help arrange the papers. Recalls having tried to hire an assistant from the New York Public Library to help her, but the woman was overwhelmed by the job and quit in frustration.

Ransom, Harry. Letter to Katherine Anne Porter. Austin, Texas, 5 Aug. 1959. 1 p. TLS. KAP Papers, BTHC (CC); KAP Papers, McL (original).

Suggests KAP use his office in the English Building; offers the assistance of a graduate student to help KAP rather than a librarian; comments on the problem with finding a suitable house in Austin.

Porter, Katherine Anne. Letter to Harry Ransom. Washington, D.C., 11 Aug. 1959. 1 p. TLS, HW address at the bottom. KAP Papers, McL (CC); KAP Papers, BTHC (original).

Writes that she cannot come to the University of Texas because of the conditions of the Ford Foundation grant; comments on the difficulty she had in reaching her decision to remain in Washington, D.C.; anticipates a future visit to Texas.

Ransom, Harry. Letter to Katherine Anne Porter. Austin, Texas, 18 Aug. 1959. 1 p. TLS. KAP Papers, BTHC (CC); KAP Papers, McL (original).

Expresses sympathy and understanding of KAP's decision not to come to the University of Texas to teach but to remain in Washington and write; comments on the KAP Library; states that the Porter Library has already received important pieces in Southern history

and literature. Comments that he hopes she is agreeable to identify-
ing her work with it to give the collection life and meaning.

Porter, Katherine Anne. Letter to Harry Ransom. Washington,
D.C., 1 Mar. 1960. 1 p. TLS. KAP Papers, McL (CC); KAP
Papers, BTHC (original).

Mentions Mr. and Mrs. Francis Biddle; comments that she is homesick for Texas and regrets postponing her semester there; mentions
health problems and her plans to visit Mexico as a representative of
the State Department from June 1 to 5.

Ransom, Harry. Letter to Katherine Anne Porter. Austin, Texas,
10 Mar. 1960. 1 p. TLS. KAP Papers, BTHC (CC); KAP
Papers, McL (original).

States that the University of Texas is deprived by not having KAP
there as writer in residence.

Ransom, Harry. Telegram to Katherine Anne Porter and Little,
Brown, & Co. Austin, Texas, 2 Apr. 1962. KAP Papers, McL.

Sends congratulations to KAP on the publishing of *Ship of Fools,* from
the Katherine Anne Porter Collection in the Academic Center.

Ransom, Harry. Letter to Thomas F. Gossett (San Antonio,
Texas). Austin, Texas, 15 Feb. 1966. 1 p. TL, CC, T. sig. KAP
Papers, BTHC.

Acknowledges receipt of photostat of KAP's letter to the Gossetts and
expresses appreciation for allowing the University of Texas to include
the letter in the KAP collection; mentions Gossett's letters from Flannery O'Connor.

Porter, Katherine Anne. Letter to Harry Ransom. Washington,
D.C., 20 Jan. 1967. 2 pp. TLS, HW corr. KAP Papers, BTHC.

Clarifies her position regarding the article in the *Fort Worth Star-
Telegram* by John Mort; states that she had written Ransom but had
received no reply; an Austin real estate agent had refused to find her
a house to rent; the *Literary Quarterly* (*Texas Quarterly*) had abruptly
stopped her subscription; a young writer in Austin tried to use her
for publicity; and the reporter misrepresented her views. Says that
she is distressed by the reporter's misrepresentation of what she said
over the telephone; apologizes for the annoyance that this incident
has caused him; comments that it is strange to her that something

promising so much happiness could have ended so badly but that she has no resentment toward Ransom.

Ransom, Harry. Telegram to Katherine Anne Porter. Austin, Texas, 31 Jan. 1967. CC draft letter, 1 p. TL, T. sig. KAP Papers, BTHC.

Writes that he found her gracious letter and that it is the first direct message he has ever received from her; comments that her decision is quite understandable and Maryland is quite fortunate. States that the Katherine Anne Porter Library will continue to symbolize her in a unique manner.

Ransom, Harry. Letter to Katherine Anne Porter. Austin, Texas, 1 Feb. 1967. 3 pp. TLS, HW corr., photocopy. KAP Papers, BTHC.

Writes to clarify the University of Texas' position regarding the controversy on the library to be named for KAP; states that he did not receive any word directly from KAP about the disposition of her collection; congratulates the University of Maryland as the recipient of her collection.

Porter, Katherine Anne. Letter to Harry Ransom. N. add., n.d. 1 p. TLS, HW corr. KAP Papers, McL (CC); KAP Papers, BTHC (original).

Regrets that she cannot come to Texas as a writer in residence; includes details of the Ford Foundation grant; requests that she be invited back to the University of Texas; states that she will be at place of writing (Lexington, Va.) until June 1, when she will leave for Washington, D.C.

Wardlaw, Frank

Wardlaw, Frank. Letter to Katherine Anne Porter. Austin, Texas, 27 Oct. 1958. 1 p. TLS. KAP Papers, McL.

Writes that he is sending copies of Vol. 1 of the *Texas Quarterly.*

Wardlaw, Frank. Letter to Katherine Anne Porter. Austin, Texas, 20 Nov. 1958. 1 p. TLS. KAP Papers, McL.

Writes that he regrets missing KAP on her recent visit to Austin; advises her that he is sending her a copy of *Texas Quarterly,* Vol. 1, No. 1.

Porter, Katherine Anne. Letter to Frank Wardlaw. Charlottesville, Va., 26 Dec. 1958. 1 p. TLS, CC. KAP Papers, McL.

Gives the condition of her health; thanks Wardlaw for sending the copy of *Texas Quarterly;* inquires about the publication in *Texas Quarterly* of a segment of the *Ship of Fools* manuscript.

Wardlaw, Frank. Letter to Katherine Anne Porter. Austin, Texas, 30 Dec. 1958. 1 p. TLS. KAP Papers, McL (original); KAP Papers, BTHC (photocopy).

States that he does not know who sent KAP a second copy of *Texas Quarterly* but he feels that it was probably Bill Handy or Jim Meriwether; states that the manuscript of *Ship of Fools* was received, and an editorial committee is deciding on the segments to be published.

Porter, Katherine Anne. Letter to Frank Wardlaw. Lexington, Va., 24 Jan. 1959. 1 p. TLS, HW corr. KAP Papers, McL (CC); KAP Papers, BTHC (photocopy).

Requests the return of her manuscript of *Ship of Fools;* inquires if *Texas Quarterly* has found the material suitable for publication.

Wardlaw, Frank. Letter to Katherine Anne Porter. Austin, Texas, 26 Jan. 1959. 1 p. TLS. KAP Papers, BTHC (CC); KAP Papers, McL (original).

States that the *Ship of Fools* manuscript is still in the editorial committee since there is a difference of opinion over what to use; states that it is very satisfactory and promises to return it as soon as possible.

Wardlaw, Frank H. Letter to Katherine Anne Porter. Austin, Texas, 21 Apr. 1967. 1 p. TL, CC, T. sig. KAP Papers, BTHC.

Accuses KAP of deceiving herself; refers to KAP rescinding permission to use her letter regarding a book on Roy Bedichek, Walter Prescott Webb, and J. Frank Dobie. States that he is removing the disputed passage at great expense to the press; expresses disappointment in KAP's actions.

Contributors

CLEANTH BROOKS, Gray Professor of Rhetoric Emeritus at Yale University, is one of the most distinguished and influential literary critics of this century. He and his wife enjoyed a close friendship with Katherine Anne Porter for many years.

JOAN GIVNER is Professor of English at the University of Regina, Canada, and editor of the *Wascana Review.* Among her many publications are *Katherine Anne Porter: A Life* (1982) and *Katherine Anne Porter: Conversations* (1987).

DON GRAHAM, an authority on Texas writing, is J. Frank Dobie Regents Professor of American and English Literature at the University of Texas at Austin. The author and editor of numerous articles and books, he recently published *No Name on the Bullet: A Biography of Audie Murphy* (1989).

SYLVIA ANN GRIDER, a noted folklorist, is Associate Professor of Anthropology and History at Texas A&M University. Her published work focuses on the image of Texas in popular culture and related Southwestern concerns.

WILLENE HENDRICK is an independent scholar residing in Urbana, Illinois. With George Hendrick she has published three books, including *Katherine Anne Porter* (rev. ed., 1988).

PAUL PORTER, the nephew of Katherine Anne Porter, is retired and lives in Austin, Texas.

JANIS P. STOUT writes fiction as well as literary criticism; her books include *Sodoms in Eden: The City in American Fiction before 1860* (1976) and *The Journey Narrative in American Literature* (1983). She is currently Associate Dean of Liberal Arts and Professor of English at Texas A&M University.

DARLENE HARBOUR UNRUE has written *Truth and Vision in Katherine Anne Porter's Fiction* (1985) and *Understanding Katherine Anne Porter* (1988). She is Professor of English at the University of Nevada–Las Vegas.

SALLY DEE WADE teaches English at Texas A&M University. Her bibliographical research into Katherine Anne Porter's Texas connection has been widely acclaimed.

THOMAS F. WALSH, whose articles on Katherine Anne Porter have appeared in *American Literature,* the *Georgia Review,* and elsewhere, is Professor of English at Georgetown University. He is writing a book on Porter's adventures in Mexico.

Index

Individual entries in the annotated bibliography have not been indexed.

Porter, Katherine Anne, fiction and essays by (*cont.*)
78–81, 102–103; "Why She Selected 'Flowering Judas,'" 102; "The Witness," 66; "Xochimilco," 75–76
Porter, Mary Alice ("Aunt Baby"), 25, 76, 78
Porter, Mary Alice Jones (Katherine Anne's mother), 6, 9, 11, 76, 78
Porter, Newell, 100n8
Porter, Paul (Katherine Anne's nephew), xiv, 89, 97–98; recollections of Katherine Anne, 25–37
Porter Collection. *See* estate, literary, of Katherine Anne Porter
Portrait of the Artist (Joyce), 103
Pound, Ezra, 47, 103–104, 107, 109; quoted, 45
Powell, Maud, 32
Pressly, Eugene, 106
primitivism, 108
prizes, literary, 64, 117

race, in fiction of Katherine Anne Porter, 65–67
racism, in Southern fiction, 62–67
Ransom, Harry, 118–21; letter to Katherine Anne Porter, 119–21
Ransom, John Crowe, 58
Reagan, Ronald, quoted, 44
regionalism: and American language, 109; literary, 115–16
"Rope" (Porter), 102
Roseliep, Raymond, quoted, 47
Rosenkavalier, Der, 27–28
Ryan, Marjorie, 105

San Antonio, Texas, xv, xxi–xxii, 51, 86, 88
San Marcos, Texas, 88
Sarah Lawrence College, 21–22
Saratoga Springs, New York, 15, 76
Scarborough, Dorothy, xvii; *In the Land,* 61–62; *The Wind,* 61
scholars, literary, xviii–xix, xxi–xxii; and Katherine Anne Porter, 52, 55, 102–105, 118–21. See also *names of scholars*
Sewanee Review, 104

sexism: of Texas literary establishment, xvii; and women writers, 45, 47, 52
Shakespeare, William, 29; *Cymbeline,* 103
Shapiro, Karl, quoted, 46–47
Ship of Fools (Porter), 16, 45–46, 87, 98, 101n14, 102, 105; successful film, 44
Sitwell, Edith, 103–104
slavery: in Porter's fiction, 65–67; in Southern fiction, 62–63
"Source, The" (Porter), 92–93
sources, for Porter's fiction, 102–106. *See also* Porter, Katherine Anne, early life of
South: class distinctions in, 14; in Porter's fiction, 86–87
Southern Review, 20, 22n2, 28
Southwest, fiction of, 60
Stalling, Donald, 4
Stein, Gertrude, 47, 51, 107, 109; *Tender Buttons,* 61
"Stopping by Woods on a Snowy Evening" (Frost), 105
Stout, Janis P., xiv–xv; quoted, xvi
Sykes, Christopher, 107

Tate, Allen, 13, 58
Tender Buttons (Stein), 61
Tennyson, Alfred, Lord, 104
Texana, xvii
Texarkana, Texas/Arkansas, 62
Texas: in fiction, 60–64; images of, xvii–xviii; multiregionalism of, 86–87; Porter's attitude toward, xiii–xiv, xvi–xviii, xxii, 14, 17, 48–49, 58, 115–122; in Porter's fiction, 65–70, 81–82, 86–99, 98–99, 102, 115–16; stereotype of, xiii, xvii, xxii; and Western myth, 70
Texas A&M University, xiv
Texas Almanac, 3
Texas Historical Commission, xxii–xxiii
Texas Institute of Letters, xiii, xvi–xvii, 48–49, 89, 116–18
Texas Observer, 49, 115, 121
Texas the Marvellous (Winter), 64
"That Tree" (Porter), 102

Katherine Ann Porter and Texas was composed into type on a Compugraphic digital phototypesetter in twelve point Baskerville with two points of spacing between the lines. University Roman was selected for display. The book was designed by Jim Billingsley, typeset by Metricomp, Inc., printed offset by Thomson-Shore, Inc., and bound by John H. Dekker and Sons, Inc. The paper on which this book is printed carries acid-free characteristics for an effective life of at least three hundred years.

TEXAS A&M UNIVERSITY PRESS : COLLEGE STATION